D1248242

IT ALL STARTED
WITH MARX

It all started with MARX

A BRIEF AND OBJECTIVE HISTORY OF RUSSIAN COMMU-
NISM, THE OBJECTIVE BEING TO LEAVE NOT ONE STONE,
BUT MANY, UNTURNED, TO STATE THE THEORIES OF MARX
SO CLEARLY THAT THEY CAN ALMOST BE UNDERSTOOD, AND
TO SHOW HOW THESE THEORIES AND MANY OLD FRIENDS
WERE CARRIED OUT BY LENIN, TROTSKY, STALIN,
MALENKOV, KHRUSHCHEV, AND OTHERS

BY RICHARD ARMOUR

WITH PICTURES FOR THOSE UNABLE TO READ

BY *Campbell Grant*

McGRAW-HILL BOOK COMPANY, INC.

NEW YORK   TORONTO   LONDON

Library of Congress Catalog Card Number: 58–12987

First Printing, August, 1958
Second Printing, March, 1962
Third Printing, January, 1964
Fourth Printing, June, 1966
Fifth Printing, October, 1967
Sixth Printing, November, 1969

02254

ACKNOWLEDGMENT

Grateful acknowledgment is made to Ambassador Charles E. Bohlen, who relieved the author considerably when he said: "There is no expert knowledge of Russia, only varying degrees of ignorance."

CONTENTS

FOREWORD

ONCE UPON A TIME there was no such thing as Communism. People ignorantly toiled and saved, hoping to Get Ahead like the heroes in Horatio Alger's books, which they forgot were fiction. Frequently, blinded by sentimentality, they left money to their Loved Ones. When this was done on a large scale, it led to the accumulation of huge fortunes, like those of Rockefeller, Carnegie, and Ford, which some harebrained member of the younger generation was sure to squander on public libraries and housing projects.

Lacking vision, many were unable to see anything shameful about accepting the rewards of industry and thrift. Still worse, there were those who spelled the word State without a capital.[1] There were also those who believed in some sort of Deity, or at least had an uneasy feeling that there was something bigger than the Head Man. They did not know, until it was pointed out by Marx, that religion is the opium of the people and should be sold only on prescription.

Conditions were dreadful, with so much freedom and family life and churchgoing and money in the bank. Something had to be done, and quickly, or the Decline of the West would be followed by the Debacle of the East, and the North and South would come tumbling after.

[1] A particularly shocking lapse on the part of capitalists.

This book, dedicated to the proposition that all men are created, tells how a new philosophy arose to fill the void and how it swept men's minds like wildfire, burning them to a crisp. It illustrates again and again the tenacity with which a handful of selfless (and propertyless) men clung to their ideals of liberty, equality, and fratricide. It reaches a crescendo in the Era of Stalin, when it shows how a Georgian cobbler's son with a bulletproof vest could rise to the top and occupy the Master Bedroom in the Kremlin.

The author has gone to a vast number of original and unoriginal sources and has interviewed countless people who have never been to Russia. The scholarship of this book is not only beyond question but beyond belief. The reader who has been seeking a trustworthy account of Communism need go no farther.

R.A.

IT ALL STARTED
WITH MARX

CHAPTER I

KARL MARX

MOST PEOPLE identify the origin of Communism with Russia, unaware that it was invented by a German while he was in France. This German, whose name was Karl Marx, went to Paris because it was a place where a man could think freely, if not clearly. Subsequently this Leftist left the Left Bank, transferring his thinking to England. At that time England was exporting such quantities of woolen goods, walking shoes, and poems by Tennyson that it had to import social philosophers to maintain the balance of trade.[1]

[1] This is not to suggest that Queen Victoria did much to encourage atheism and free love.

How Communism got to Russia, we shall see later. It was not by surface travel but by underground.

BIRTH AND BOYHOOD

Karl Marx was born in the Rhineland city of Trier early on the morning of May 5, 1818.[1] It was an ungodly hour, which may explain Marx's later attitude toward religion. He awoke everyone with his cries, and few realized that even then he was complaining about the injustice of it all. While his father washed down a *Schnitzel* with a stein of lager, poor Karl was allowed nothing but milk, and even this he had to work for.

Karl's father was a lawyer, and he hoped his son would follow in his footsteps, which led from the house to the office to the *Bierstube*. Like a good son, Karl promised to study law, but there was a gleam in his eye which handicapped him when it came to reading fine print.[2] He was a pale, studious lad with a philosophical bent, long hours at a desk having ruined his posture. Even in adolescence he was so busy reading that his morals were beyond reproach. Only once did his parents have to pay a small fine to get him out of trouble, and that was for an overdue book.

UNIVERSITY CAREER

At the University of Bonn, which Karl attended in order to revolutionize the curriculum, an event of no little importance occurred. He engaged in a duel and, momentarily preoccupied with a philosophical problem, lowered his guard. He received a thrust over the left (*sic*) eye, which marked him for life.

About this time Karl began to write poetry and invented free verse, a form which he found suited to writing about free love. It is interesting to speculate about the effect on world politics and the sonnet had he made poetry his career. Since he did not, we have at least been spared recitations from *The*

[1] Whether it was two o'clock, as stated by E. H. Carr, or one-thirty, as maintained by B. Nicolaievsky and O. Maenchen-Helfen, is a controversy from which we prefer to remain aloof.

[2] Possibly caused by overstudy at the little red schoolhouse.

Selected Poems of Karl Marx by millions of unhappy school-children.

After a year at Bonn, young Marx went to Berlin University, ostensibly to pursue the law, which was running scared. But he seems to have taken a wrong turn at one of the corridors, and his notebooks were full of Aristotle, Spinoza, Leibnitz, and Bacon, the latter in long strips used as bookmarks.

INFLUENCE OF HEGEL

It was at this time that he became a Hegelian, firmly asserting that nothing is static, even when his hair stood on end and you could plainly see sparks. Everything, he insisted, was flowing. To prove this he would go around turning on faucets. It was from Hegel that he got the idea of "dialectic," which has been lucidly defined as "the triadic movement of thought from thesis to antithesis to synthesis." [1] However, the idea of "dialectical materialism" is Marx's very own. Those who have borrowed it have always been glad to give it back.

Because of a disagreement with one of his professors, who refused to sit in the back row while Marx lectured to the class, Karl withdrew rather hastily from Berlin University. A week later he took his doctorate at the University of Jena. [2] It must have been a busy week, during which he met all the requirements, [3] such as drinking a certain number of liters of beer and waltzing with the wife of the *Rektor*. At any rate he was now entitled to be called Dr. Marx, though not encouraged to perform appendectomies.

JOURNALISM AND JENNY

After winning his degree, Marx went home long enough to have a violent quarrel with his mother over finances. She made

[1] W. T. Jones, *A History of Western Philosophy,* p. 1016. The author shrewdly tells us that "we must distinguish between Marx's heart and his head." This should not be too difficult, since one is inside and the other outside.

[2] Unbelievable as it is, this is the truth, which cannot be said of some of the other unbelievable statements in this book.

[3] Or someone of influence.

Waltzing with the Rektor's wife

the mistake of saying that he was a big boy now and should have his allowance reduced. Not as yet having coined the phrase, "to each according to his need," Marx stormed off to Bonn. In this very religious city, he had the brilliant idea of founding a *Journal of Atheism,* which, because of lack of competition, was certain of success. However, he was unable to convince others of this golden opportunity and gave up in disgust.

Feeling himself in bad odor, he went to Cologne. There he became editor of a radical newspaper. Soon he was widely known for his articles defending the freedom of the press, writing them with his right hand while blue-penciling his reporters' articles with his left.

Finally the paper folded (it had been only slightly crumpled before), and Marx left for Paris. At the station to see him off were a dozen or so of his creditors, shaking their fists at him in what later came to be recognized as the Communist salute.

Before leaving Cologne, Marx married Jenny von Westphalen, resolutely overlooking the fact that she came of a wealthy family and he was out of work. They had been engaged for seven years, which demonstrates how Marx sometimes quailed before a Great Decision. But now he was hungry.

4

They had an idyllic honeymoon, during which Marx filled five large notebooks with extracts from his reading. Their relationship grew in intimacy as Jenny turned his pages and sharpened his pencils.

In Paris, Marx wrote for a revolutionary German-language paper, *Vorwärts*,[1] which was largely ignored by the good citizens of Paris, most of whom did not own a German-French dictionary. Every evening he plotted and schemed in smoke-filled rooms, where he developed a dim view of the future.

Smokers in a plot-filled room

According to one biographer, "Marx's journalistic pen was dipped in gall."[2] When one of Marx's articles advocated murdering the King of Prussia, many thought this was going too far. Why not murder the King of France, who was close by? The king, Louis Philippe, grew uneasy at this sort of talk, closed down the paper, and ordered Marx to leave Paris within twenty-four hours. Marx intended to settle somewhere outside the city limits, but left with such a burst of speed that his momentum carried him all the way to Belgium.

PERSONAL APPEARANCE

Marx soon became a familiar figure in Brussels. His large head, short legs, and square trunk made a lasting impression,

[1] *Forward*, a journal that was always in the van, at least while being delivered.

[2] Someone used the wrong bottle when filling his inkwell.

especially on his mattress. Failing to gain average height,[1] he had grown a bushy, untrimmed beard to hide his disappointment. During years of poverty, it kept his throat and chest warm and saved him the price of a scarf. Only his wife, who died without revealing his secret, knew whether he ever wore a tie or, indeed, had a neck.[2]

About this time Marx stopped going to a barber, being unable to sit there and listen while someone else talked. So his hair grew down over his ears and neck and mingled with his beard, setting a style for spies, revolutionaries, poets, and makers of cough drops.

COLLABORATION WITH ENGELS

Marx was joined in Brussels by Friedrich Engels, his friend and co-worker.[3] Engels thought Marx was a genius, and Marx agreed. Everywhere Marx went, Engels tagged right behind

[1] The *sine qua non* of a Communist leader. See Lenin, Trotsky, Stalin, and Khrushchev below.

[2] Marx may have been a white collar worker, but because of his beard the laborers never knew.

[3] Engels was not only Marx's lifetime friend but virtually his only friend. Marx was too busy improving the lot of mankind to care much about people.

Engels records the word

The master's shadow

him. The only time Engels became a nuisance was when the two of them went through a revolving door together or crowded into a phone booth.

Engels was severely handicapped by being the son of a textile industrialist, but at least learned to tell a spindle from a spinster. Marx, on the other hand, did not see a worker up close until he was in his thirties, and even then in meetings and not in factories. He found it easier to understand workers if he kept away from them, and could visualize their problems better if he never saw them. After all, Marx was a philosopher, and it was hard for him to think if he got tangled up with reality. It is true that he often got his hands grimy and black, but that was from changing his typewriter ribbon.

REVOLUTIONARY IDEAS

Increasingly Marx came to feel that the world must be changed and that he was the man for the job. Humanity must be freed from three besetting evils: (1) marriage, (2) religion, and (3) private property. Since Marx had no religion and no private property, he himself was in pretty good shape. As for

7

marriage, it may be significant that most of those who sub-
scribed to the Marx-Engels conviction that marriage *must* be
done away with were married men.[1]

All about him Marx saw class struggle. In economic life it
was between the proletariat and the bourgeoisie. In schools it
was between pupils and teachers.[2] Marx thought something

Class struggle

could be done to improve the position of the proletariat, which
at that time was prone. The best way to help the proletariat,
or working class, was to do away with the bourgeoisie,[3] or
property-owning class. What qualified Marx for his proletariat
(he already had his baccalaureate) was the work he did with
his hands. Bending over a desk in the public library, he lifted
ideas out of books from morning till night.

Marx wanted a classless society. He was absolutely on the
level about this. He also wished to substitute labor for money,

[1] The opinion of their wives has not been recorded. It is probable that
Jenny, who several times was on the verge of a nervous breakdown, would
have been against it too.

[2] Education was then at the crossroads, where it still is.

[3] Not to mention the petty bourgeoisie, who were frightfully small about
money matters.

which would make banks and cash registers unnecessary and counterfeiting impossible. Unfortunately, he could never figure out how to make change when he wanted to buy an article that cost only ten minutes' work and the smallest thing he had on him was an hour.

Marx was a visionary and could look far into the future, though he was not a 20-20 visionary. For instance he foresaw a time when the State would "wither away," leaving nothing

The position of the proletariat

but a few dried-up civil service employees forgotten at their posts. What he did not see, perhaps because of a speck on his spectacles, was a State that instead of withering grew and grew-some more.

At any rate Marx set out to give the laboring class a chance to suffer in a new way. He spread his doctrine far and wide, and sometimes spread it pretty thin. When he was not lecturing, he wrote feverishly.[1] He had a genius for being pithy. Frequently he could boil down a simple idea and state it in 400 pages.

[1] He did his best writing when he had a temperature of 102 degrees or over. Sometimes, we are told, he wrote "at a white heat," and must have been a really sick man.

THE COMMUNIST MANIFESTO

In 1847 the Communists held a convention in London. They came from all over Europe, equipped with expense accounts, noisemakers, and pocket flasks, each determined to be the life of the Party. Many wore lapel buttons with such slogans as "I Like Marx" and "Down With Everybody." Needing something to discuss, a nostrum for the rostrum, they asked Marx to prepare them a platform, suitably heavy and wooden.

So it was that Marx wrote *The Communist Manifesto*. Its most memorable part is the opening sentence: "A specter is haunting Europe—the specter of Communism." Obviously Marx hoped by this transparent device to attract readers of ghost stories and make inroads on the Edgar Allan Poe market.

The use of the term "Communist" in the *Manifesto* helped make the word popular, especially among Communists. Indeed the League of the Just, to which Marx belonged, changed its name to the Communist League, possibly because of jibes about "Just what?" From the closing sentences of the *Manifesto* the Communists devised their stirring motto: "Workers of the world, unite! You have nothing to lose but your chains!" Though in some instances their chains were heirlooms, handed down for generations, they were willing to make the sacrifice.

In 1848, Marx was contributing to several newspapers as well as to the general unrest. Because of this he was given 24 hours to leave Brussels. The order to leave caught him napping. By the time he awoke, there was no chance to gather up such personal effects as his toothbrush, his washcloth, or his wife. He particularly regretted leaving behind his straight razor, which had been in the family for years and was a well-tempered blade.

After a brief sojourn in Paris he went on to Cologne, where he edited another radical paper and hatched plots. This latter was difficult for Marx, a nervous man who seldom sat long in one spot. However, he persevered for the good of the Cause, and was notably effective in making the bourgeoisie and the proletariat see the antagonism which had existed for years between them, unnoticed.

But now Marx was given 23 hours to leave Germany. By this time he was adept at living out of a suitcase, and needed only to snap the latches. Back to Paris he went. After only one month he was asked to leave in 22 hours. They were tightening

23 hours to leave

up on him. His picture appeared in post offices and government buildings, marked Unwanted. A philosopher by trade,[1] he took this philosophically. Besides, it gave him a new Communist slogan: Join the Party and See the World.

Marx had only two places left to go—England or prison. Through an anguished night he was torn by Indecision and tormented by Doubt. At the last minute [2] he decided on England, fearful that the dampness of the Paris dungeon might aggravate his rheumatism. Apparently no one had told him about English weather.

MARX IN ENGLAND

He arrived in London in a fog. Soon he was joined by his wife and three (later six) children, who were intensely loyal to him and had no place else to go. Paradoxically, though he was a poor provider, he was a man who would make his mark.[3] Instead of reassuring his family with "Wait till my ship comes in," he would say, with confidence, "Come the revolution. . . ."

In London Marx spent the second half of his life attending meetings of secret societies. Some of these were so secret that he was never told their names or where they met, and therefore often arrived late. Most of the members put on false beards to disguise themselves. Since Marx's beard was the real thing, disguise posed a problem. He solved it by parting his beard in the middle and slicking down his hair.

At this time he was also the brains behind a new organization, the International Working Men's Association, although certain rules about being a worker had to be waived before Marx himself could become a member.

Marx went from place to place lecturing on economics. He had to keep moving, because he was being closely watched by the authorities, especially the authorities on economics. During his university career he had majored in law and philosophy, but

[1] There is no evidence, however, that he made any attempt to found a trade union for philosophers.

[2] I.e., after 21 hours and 59 minutes.

[3] The mark was then worth about twenty cents.

12

he had once overheard a conversation about the law of supply and demand and felt qualified to lecture on it. It must have been a relief to Marx that his audiences were mostly made up of working men who knew nothing whatever about the subject, being too busy earning a living to read up on how they were doing it. Marx, having no regular work, had ample time to read the great economists like John Stuart Mill and Adam Smith, most of whom were similarly unemployed.[1]

Marx's disguise

A FAMILY SCENE

For some years the Marxes lived at No. 28 Dean Street, Soho. There was a close feeling in the Marx family, for Karl and Jenny, along with their six children and a nurse, lived in two small rooms. The place had a cozy, lived-in look.

Marx dearly loved to tell his children bedtime stories. While Jenny was getting their beds ready by removing the paper and inkwells, Marx, with three children on each knee, entertained them with such stories as "The Bourgeois Cat and the Prole-

---

[1] "Only on one recorded occasion during the whole of Marx's 30 years' stay in England," states one authority, "did he attempt to find regular employment." Apparently it was an entirely distasteful experience.

tarian Mouse," "Snow White and the Seven Trade Unionists," and their favorite, "Little Red Riding Hood." How they loved to hear him describe Little Red Riding Hood, a poor working girl, and her grandmother, a downtrodden peasant woman. How they screamed with fright when he got down on his hands and knees and acted out the part of the capitalist wolf, trying to exploit Little Red and Granny. But the story always ended happily. The Revolution came, in the nick of time, and the wolf went down in a hail of hammers and sickles. It was great fun, though the children were sometimes so excited that they could not go to sleep for hours, and Marx himself had to walk the London streets to get a grip on himself.

FOREIGN CORRESPONDENT

In the 1850s Marx contributed to the *New York Tribune,* as Republicans would like to forget. The editor was the famous Horace Greeley. His advice, "Go west, young man," was completely lost on Marx, who never ventured beyond London's West End.

Marx specialized in writing vividly about wars and revolutions, though he was unable to see anything of them unless they took place in the street in front of the British Museum. It was there that he wrote his masterful eyewitness accounts of the Turko-Russian War. His dispatches [1] invariably got to New York before those written by impractical reporters in the Near East, who had a penchant for realism.

Marx was paid five dollars an article by the *Tribune.* He considered himself underpaid, and this increased his annoyance with capitalism. Since he would have starved to death without this income, the *Tribune* might have saved the world from Communism by either paying Marx nothing or paying him more.

POVERTY AND DISAPPOINTMENT

In his later years Marx was very poor. But for the money from the *Tribune* and gifts from Engels, who had reluctantly

[1] Which, as is sometimes forgotten, were bitterly anti-Russian.

14

inherited a cotton mill, he would have been unable to buy paper and pencil.[1] The Marx-Engels correspondence is full of long, involved letters by Marx concerning economic philosophy, usually centering on such basic questions as "Where is my money?" Marx's exploitation of Engels is an interesting reversal of Marxist theory. In this instance a proletarian exploited a bourgeois.

Always Marx was waiting for the capitalistic world to collapse. Each morning he would throw off the covers and leap from bed crying, "Workers of the world, arise!" Then he would run to get the newspaper, goose-pimply with anticipation, hoping for a headline such as "Western World Collapses" or "Bubonic Plague Carries Off Millions of Capitalists."

Unfortunately nothing horrible happened, no catastrophe oc-

[1] He had long since given up food and drink.

Pshaw! Good news again!

15

curred. Indeed the only really gloomy articles he found that cheered him up were those he had written himself.

Marx's fondest dream was of a great war with long casualty lists made up of bourgeoisie who had stupidly enlisted to protect their property. The proletariat, having no such motive, would of course not enlist, and the intellectuals, like Marx, would have bad eyesight from excessive reading and be exempt from the draft. But war stubbornly refused to break out, and Marx grew terribly despondent. *"Gott im Himmel,"* he would exclaim, unembarrassed at having invoked a nonexistent Deity, "when will this *furchtbar* peace come to an end?"

Thus it was that he took great joy in the outbreak of the Franco-Prussian War in 1870. As its bloody battles raged, taking a heavy toll of capitalists and anyone else who got in the way of a bullet, Marx became the happiest man alive. But the war came to an early end, alas, with the defeat of Napoleon III at the Battle of Sedan, and Marx was again plunged into gloom.

DAS KAPITAL

All this time Marx was writing his *magnum opus*. This was *Das Kapital,* the first volume of which appeared in 1867, when Marx was almost fifty and afflicted with neuralgia, pleurisy, and middle age. It is not, as many suppose, a treatise on punctuation. Nor is it a guidebook to the historic sights of Berlin. Engels called it "the Bible of the working classes," perhaps because it was the Genesis of Communism and (he hoped) the Exodus of Capitalism.

In this famous work Marx propounded his doctrine of class struggle and his "theory of change." This latter was his belief that, over the centuries, the bourgeoisie had slyly made change in such a way as to impoverish the gullible proletariat. Even more revolutionary was his "theory of surplus value," whereby he declared that all capitalists are surplus and of value only to themselves. In *Das Kapital* Marx discusses money at great length. Never having had much of it, this gave him a certain vicarious pleasure.[1]

Marx did not live to complete *Das Kapital*, nor have many people lived to finish reading it. However, it was continued by his friend Engels, who made use of Marx's papers, both daily and Sunday, and faithfully carried out his master's wishes.[2] After the work got up to three thick volumes, Engels died, having overtaxed his heart by lifting all three at once.[3] The world awaits the eight-page condensation of *Das Kapital*, to be called *Daskap*, which *The Reader's Digest* has long had under way.

ILLNESS AND DEATH

In his final years Marx suffered from acute mental depression, no doubt because peace kept hanging on and there was no sign of a rift in the black pall of prosperity. Afflicted by headaches and insomnia, not to mention polemics and a bad case of diatribes, he became bedridden.[4] The happy days in the British Museum were over.

But he continued his studies to the end, working out a technique whereby anything involved and unclear would be taken as profound. This technique came to be known as Marxmanship, and was an early predecessor of Gamesmanship.

Finally, on March 14, 1883, the Father of Communism died. He left behind him some of the most significant books in the field of philosophy and economics, most of them borrowed from the library and long overdue.

The influence of Marx being, as one scholar states, "incalculable," we shall make no attempt to calculate it.

[1] Cf. the famous comment attributed to Marx's mother: "I wish Karl had spent his time making capital instead of writing about it."

[2] As well as beer bottles and dirty dishes.

[3] Instead of being the kind of book that is hard to put down, it is the kind that is hard to pick up.

[4] Marx had, or thought he had, an enlarged liver, piles, carbuncles, pernicious anemia, consumption, apoplexy, and assorted nervous disorders. He was either a hypochondriac or distinctly unwell.

CHAPTER II

RUSSIA BEFORE
THE REVOLUTION

DURING ALL HIS YEARS of theorizing, Marx seems to have turned his back on Russia, a dangerous thing to do. The best opportunity for social upheaval, he thought, was in highly industrialized countries, where, in crowded factories, capital and labor would be at each other's throats, rubbing Adam's apples until irritation was inevitable.

But Marx, never having been a farmer, failed to realize that factories are not a fertile field. Had he lived longer, he would have been amazed to see that the ideas which he sowed between rows of machinery in Germany and England came up in the broad farmlands of Russia. What carried the seeds of revolt to Russia? Secret couriers? Prevailing winds? Birds?

At any rate, Russia was overdue for a revolution. France, Germany, and Italy had had at least one a century, and Russia was dragging her feet revolutionwise. Let us briefly survey the history of Russia, dwelling only on matters of the utmost irrelevance, and see why the Time was Ripe, in 1888, for the Revolution of 1917.

THE LAND

Modern Russia, which occupies more than one-sixth of the land surface of the world, is so large that it slops over from Europe into Asia and vice versa. The two parts are separated by such natural barriers as mountains, rivers, and dotted lines. From earliest times the Russian has had plenty of elbow room, which explains why he puts his hands on his hips when dancing. Vast forests have provided lumber and fuel as well as a place to hide from secret police and weekend guests. The long winter nights have led to a morbid fear of insomnia. Despite great wealth of natural resources, there has always been a shortage of certain articles, such as "the" and "a." [1]

COMING OF THE SLAVS

The ancestors of the modern Russians were Slavs, which is why the Russians do not go in for ancestor worship. Other nomadic races, such as the Vikings and the Mongols, penetrated the vast land that was later to become Russia, but "all of them were absorbed by the Slavs," whose skin was no doubt in great demand for use as blotting paper.

Indeed some anthropologists and archeologists believe that the Garden of Eden may have been in what is now the southern part of Russia. If true, this would mean that Adam and Eve,.

---

[1] For which there are no words in Russian.

who were banished without due process of law, were the first of a long line of Displaced Persons.

Passing quickly over the Scythians, Sarmatians, and other early settlers about whom little is known,[1] we return regretfully to the Slavs, who since last mentioned have spread through the wide plains from the Elbe to the Volga and from the Dnieper to the Danube.[2] As they overran Russia, the Slavs took with them not only their customs and costumes but their language. Thus it is that the Slavic tongue can be recognized in Russia today, being somewhat thick in the back and inclined to curl at the tip.[3]

NEXT THE VIKINGS

In the ninth century the Slavs invited the Vikings, under the leadership of Rurik, to come south for the winter and join them in sports and social activities, such as fighting the Turks. The Vikings, whose spears were growing rusty from disuse, accepted

[1] By the author.

[2] Another river we can think of, in fact have trouble getting out of our mind, is the Bug.

[3] Next time a Slav sticks out his tongue at you, take a look.

The Slavs invited the Vikings

with Alacrity. (Rurik's second cousin.) So quickly did they arrive that the Slavs called them "Rush" or "Russ," which some think is the origin of the word "Russian."

Rurik was followed by Oleg, known as Oleg the Bowleg because of his many years in the saddle. Returning from a campaign against the Khazars, he found that his favorite horse had died while he was away. Standing, helmet in hand, by the skeleton of his horse near the River Volga, Oleg decided to change the main stream of history by switching Russian trade to the Dnieper. He thus became the first ruler to change streams in midhorse.

After Oleg came Svyatoslav, who called himself Svyatoslav the Great, no doubt to distinguish himself from all the other Svyatoslavs. According to his biographer, he was "a hearty campaigner whose saddle was his pillow." No sooner did his head hit the saddle than he was sound asleep, and it terrified the enemy to hear him snoring as his horse galloped across the battlefield.

Svyatoslav asleep in the saddle

Under such memorable rulers as Vladimir I, Yaroslav (called "The Wise" by one of his retainers, who was no fool himself), and Vladimir Monomach ("Mac" to his intimates), Russia expanded. Vladimir was famous as a hunter, and is said to have been "thrown by a bull, bitten by a bear, and borne to the ground by a wolf." In those days a monarch wasn't tied to his desk but could get out into the woods and have some fun.

A Slavic social event

22

In the thirteenth century Russia was harassed by the Tartars, who swept in from the east and threatened to replace Russian dressing with Tartar sauce. The Tartars, led by Genghis Khan, were a tough lot.[1] "A week afield with nothing to eat but mare's milk and blood," says one historian, "was common practice," especially by those on an ulcer diet. Mare's milk was sometimes in short supply, but blood was always plentiful.

A Tartar pauses for his spot of mare's milk

The Tartars exacted a tribute of one skin per year from each household, and many a family must have had trouble deciding whose to give up.

One of the Russian heroes of this period was Alexander Nevsky. Against a superior force of Germans, this shrewd warrior picked as his battleground the frozen Lake Peipus. The

---

[1] Cf. the well-known saying, "Scratch a Russian and find a Tartar." What you would have found if you had scratched a Tartar we can only imagine.

Germans got cold feet and fled westward with sniffles and chilblains.[1]

The end of the Tartar threat came in the 1390s, when Tamerlane,[2] or Timur the Lame, after sweeping across Asia and threatening to take Moscow, for some reason turned south and east to India. Why he led his horde on this curving route is not known, though he may have been favoring his game leg. At any rate he set out for Russia and wound up in India, whereas Columbus set out for India and wound up in America, a parallel which may help to explain Mr. Nehru's neutralism.

THE KREMLIN, ETC.

Toward the end of the fourteenth century, after the Tartar menace passed,[3] one Dmitry Donskoi ordered a great stone wall, called the Kremlin, to be built. Aware that stone walls do

[1] Some consider this the original Cold War.

[2] Also Timurlane and Tamberlaine. Historians are uncertain spellers at best.

[3] A careful reading of history reveals no instance of a scholar ever having said anything good about the Tartars, among whom there must surely have been some decent chaps.

Suitable additions to the Kremlin

not a prison make, subsequent rulers made such suitable additions as dungeons, torture chambers, knout racks, and bins for storing spare skulls. Equally important, under Ivan III[1] in 1472, was adoption of the double-headed eagle as Russia's coat of arms. This came about when Ivan discovered that two heads are better than one, especially when they face in opposite directions and your enemies don't know whether you are coming or going.

It was in the time of Dmitry that, as one historian puts it, "The Russians found a ford and crossed the Don." If true, this not only substantiates the claim that a Russian invented the automobile in the Middle Ages but indicates that an early model was virtually waterproof.

IVAN THE TERRIBLE

With only a brief mention of the twenty-eight-year reign of Basil III, who really did marry a Lithuanian woman named Helen Glinsky, we come with no little pleasure to Basil's son, Ivan IV, called Ivan the Severe by those given to understatement but Ivan the Terrible by most. He was mistreated as a boy, being kept cooped up in the castle when he wanted to be out ice-skating. When he came to the throne, he executed everyone who had been unkind to him in his youth, and for a generation thereafter Russia was sparsely populated. Interestingly enough, he was the first Russian ruler to call himself "Tsar." He had intended to make it "Caesar," but his tongue got caught in his teeth.

Ivan was given to fits of fury. In one of these he struck his favorite son with a steel-tipped staff, killing him. Afterward he was remorseful, having intended only to batter the lad into insensibility. He is not known to have killed any of his wives, although he had six or seven and therefore exceptional opportunity. He won one of them in a chess game,[2] his moral prin-

[1] Ivan was related by marriage to Emperor Constantine Paleolog, who, we are told, "died fighting in his walls." How he got in there and what he was doing, unless battling termites, remains a fascinating mystery.

[2] The original check mate.

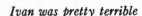

ciples preventing him from playing for money. Ivan finally died of a stroke.[1]

The Russian line, going back to Rurik, finally came to an end, but not until after a little difficulty with the so-called False Dmitri, who claimed to be a son of Ivan and acted almost as Terrible. Eventually Dmitri was killed, and his body was burned and the ashes shot from a cannon to make sure he was dead. A strong strain of skepticism runs through the Russian character.

Boris Godunov, a commoner, but no commoner than most, was crazy to be Czar.[2] At first he pretended not to want the throne, but his supporters insisted. "What's Godunov for us," they said, "is Godunov for anybody." Shortly after being made Czar by popular acclaim, Boris became hated by everyone, and it is no wonder that popular elections lost their popularity with Russian rulers.

[1] Of luck, for his subjects.
[2] An excellent, if not essential, qualification. With a little more insanity, he might have been thought to have royal blood.

About this time the Romanov dynasty began. Michael Romanov, the first of the line, thought he ruled divinely.[1] His son, Alexis, who was more interested in hawking than in running the government, went around with a fierce bird on his wrist that watched him like a hawk. Alexis, in his time, had to put up with some grumbling by the serfs, who were rather disagreeable about starving to death. But he made a substantial contribution to this period of Russian history, known as the Time of Trouble.

Modern Russia began, however, with Peter the Great (1672–1725), who personally cut the beards off his nobles to make them look like Europeans.[2] When they still looked too much like Russians, he cut their heads off. Peter liked to keep busy.

[1] I.e., by Divine Right.

[2] Beards could be worn only by those who paid a tax on them, and it was hard to smuggle a beard past a revenuer.

"What else might come off?"

He built up the Russian Army and the Russian Navy, defeated Sweden and Turkey, slew plotters with his own hand (in which he held a sword), edited the first newspaper to make sure of getting a good press, and built a window to Europe where he sat by the hour looking through binoculars until he became known as Peeping Pete.[1]

During the forty-three years of Peter's reign, according to a trustworthy historian, "the serfs had no voice," apparently afflicted with chronic laryngitis. But the serfs worried Peter less than the Cossacks. These were trick horsemen who could gallop up the steppes and right into the palace. We are told that they carried off women and livestock, perhaps a comely wench under one arm and a comely cow under the other. Sometimes they put villages to the torch; other times they did it the easy way, putting the torch to villages.

ERA OF CATHERINE THE GREAT

Passing over Peter the Great's successors, such as Peter II, Catherine (the Lesser), and Elizabeth, who died with a glass of cherry brandy at her lips,[2] we come to Catherine the Great. Catherine had four secretaries to make sure she was never late to a rendezvous. According to one of her biographers, "she kept her castoff lovers as friends," which is an indication of her sentimental regard for souvenirs. Moreover, they formed a sort of ready reserve. Under Catherine, whose weight was considerable, Russia spread, taking in the Crimea and part of Poland.

Then, during the reign of Catherine's grandson, Alexander I, Napoleon posed a threat. However, Napoleon and Alexander signed a treaty of friendship (see Hitler and Stalin, below) which was to last forever. Shortly before the expiration date, Napoleon led his army into Russia. In the winter campaign that followed, Napoleon learned the strategic value of long marches and long underwear and came out ahead. That is, he

[1] He also simplified the alphabet and picked up a bit of dentistry, which he practiced on his friends.

[2] A pleasant way to go.

came out ahead of Alexander, who chased him all the way back to Paris.[1]

LAST OF THE ROMANOVS

The Romanov dynasty was beginning to show signs of wear and tear. Nicholas I, though firmly in the saddle, had feet of clay, which tended to cake in the stirrups. Even the horses were beginning to notice. Alexander II, hoping to be remembered as the Abraham Lincoln of Russia although he looked ridiculous in a stovepipe hat, liberated the serfs, giving each a piece of land too small to live on. But being a do-good did no good for Alex. He was blown up by terrorists who didn't think he was moving fast enough.

Alexander III, the father of the last Czar, is said to have taken "the long view of Russia," i.e., from St. Petersburg to Vladivostok. He believed in "Russia for the Russians," which was easy because conditions were so bad that no one else wanted the place. Food was short, and so were millions of undernourished peasants. Once the train in which Alexander was riding was blown off the tracks, and not by high winds.

The last and noblest Romanov them all was Nicholas II, who looked so much like King George V of England that they were often mistaken, though Nicholas was mistaken more often than George. His coronation festivities were a riot, several hundred persons being trampled to death when the peasants insisted on dancing with their boots on.[2] He thus became known as "Bloody Nicholas," a nickname he really earned only at the close of his career, when he was perforated by Bolshevik bullets.

Russia took part in two wars during the reign of Nicholas, losing to Japan in 1905 and doing none too well against Germany in World War I. War was getting unpopular, and so was the Czar. Bombs, we are told, "began to fly," though most were still the old-fashioned kind that had to be thrown. Many

---

[1] Napoleon called Alexander "The Sphinx of the North." Alexander, in turn, called Napoleon "The Beast." Neither believed in flattery.

[2] They died that way, too.

George and Nicholas: "Your face is familiar."

were left under chairs and tables, and not because their owners were forgetful.

Nicholas wasn't helped much by Rasputin, a rascally monk whom someone has called "the axle on which revolved the destinies of Russia." Anyhow, he was a big wheel. Rasputin, who held the Czarina in the palm of his hand,[1] believed that sin was necessary to salvation, and did all he could to see that everyone was saved. Though no Marxist, he was nonetheless enthusiastic about free love, insisting that the best things in life are free.[2] He was finally murdered by a group of conservative noblemen who believed in paying their way. They had to poison him, shoot him, and drown him before he gave up. Then he died of a broken heart, suddenly aware of his unpopularity.

Russia had been ready for the Revolution of 1917 for some time, and now that it was 1917 it could be postponed no longer. The curtain was about to go up on one of the Great Dramas of History, and pacing nervously in the wings was an obscure actor named Nicolai V. Lenin.

[1] The Czarina never got her growth.
[2] He had long championed the free press (i.e., squeeze).

Rasputin was hard to kill

CHAPTER III

LENIN

LENIN, who put Marx's theories into practice, was born in Simbirsk on the Volga on April 22, 1870. He was named Vladimir Ilyich Ulianov and thus had something to revolt against from the very beginning.[1] As a baby, Vladimir had a bald, domelike head to which, in later life, he added a mustache and pointed beard to prove that if he couldn't grow hair one place he could grow it another.[2]

[1] His mother, we might mention in passing, was the daughter of a physician named Alexander Blank, who was afflicted with amnesia and unable to remember his last name.

[2] He also hoped to foil amateur artists who add mustaches and beards to pictures in the Moscow subway.

Vladimir's father, Ilya Ulianov, was a provincial school-teacher. A stern, righteous man, he was conservative in politics and devoutly religious. Fortunately he died too early to know how his son turned out. Vladimir's mother brought up the family, the members of which, we are told, "remained intimately bound to one another." It was a pretty sight to see them going to church, like a party of mountain climbers, with Maria Alexandrovna, the mother, resolutely at the head and little Vladimir dragging along behind, his heels digging a furrow in the rich black soil of his native land.

EARLY TENDENCIES

Vladimir worshiped his older brother, Alexander, who was a terror in his youth and a terrorist when he reached manhood. Alexander plotted to assassinate the Czar but was caught red-handed, and hanged. Vladimir, who had counted on receiving his brother's castoff clothing for some years, was understandably upset.

He took to reading *Das Kapital*. This he did in the kitchen, probably because reading about poverty made him hungry and he wanted to be where he could grab a bite of *kavkaski shasslik* before starting the next chapter. His sister Anna has given us a vivid description of the young scholar at work. "Sitting on the kitchen stove . . . and making violent gesticulations," she writes, "he would tell me with burning enthusiasm about the principles of Marxist theory. . . ." As his enthusiasm burst into flames, no doubt his gesticulations became wilder and his screams louder, until Anna pulled him down from the stove and dropped him in the sink.[1] But for Anna, Communism might have lost a great leader.

STUDENT OF LAW

Vladimir entered Kazan University in October, 1887, and was expelled in December of the same year. Something he had done was displeasing to the authorities, possibly his use of

[1] In a footnote on the next page Lenin's biographer writes: "Lenin started to smoke at this time."

laboratory periods to assemble bombs which he lobbed into the dean's residence. It was suggested that he might do better elsewhere, though by his rather special standards he seemed to be doing well enough at old K.U.

At good old K.U.

A period ensued when Vladimir studied law at home. He read assiduously and, unhampered by professors, made rapid progress. Many days he would trudge off into the woods, loaded down with legal treatises, and not come home until evening. It is assumed that he was studying law in some solitary spot, though he may have been bird-watching.

Eventually Vladimir took the law examinations at St. Petersburg University and passed with flying colors.[1] His mother hoped he would now join the Moscow branch of some big Wall Street firm, but his brief practice was not such as to attract outside offers. "He acted for the defendants in a few petty criminal cases," says one admiring biographer, "and in every instance lost." The local jail was beginning to bulge with his clients.

[1] Without ever attending. See Marx and his Ph.D. at Jena, above. This sort of thing naturally makes Communism popular with students.

34

It was not malpractice of the law, however, that led to his imprisonment, but the pursuit of his avocation, which was inciting revolt. Closing his law office, he went underground, taking with him the complete works of Marx and a large supply of candles. His revolutionary tendencies became known throughout St. Petersburg, and every time he lifted a manhole cover he was shadowed by the secret police, who thus deprived him of the healthful benefits of sunshine. They rightly suspected him of being responsible for such inflammatory slogans on walls and fences as "Two pants with every suit!" "Two suits with every pants!" and "The Tsar is a tsap!" The fact that he was usually carrying a brush and a bucket of red paint confirmed their suspicions.

The first time he was arrested it was for crossing the frontier with a double-bottomed suitcase [1] full of illegal literature, the precise nature of which we do not know. He may only have been trafficking in French postcards and slightly soiled novels.

[1] As one of the border guards quipped (twice): "Let's get to the bottom of this."

Going underground

His jailers were sensitive types who did not appreciate the traces of his former environment, the sewer. To clean him up and make a shining example of him, they washed their dirty Lenin in public.

Determined and resourceful, Lenin was not to be stopped by mere humiliation. While in prison, he wrote pamphlets and books in invisible ink, despite the almost unbelievable difficulty of proofreading. When the supply of foolscap was exhausted, he ingeniously pricked holes in toilet paper with a pin, hoping his confederates outside would know enough to put it on a player piano. After fourteen months of pamphleteering, during which he occasionally had to swallow a handful of pins to avoid detection, Lenin was released from prison and banished for three years to Siberia.

He rather enjoyed Siberia, for he had time to read and write [1] and dream about revolution. Often he played chess with peasants whom he taught the rudiments of the game but not the fine points. Wild game grew unafraid of him and would often lick the top of his head, seeking salt. Once he and a fox—he felt a certain kinship for foxes—stood staring at each other until Lenin dropped his eyes in embarrassment. The stark beauty of Siberia appealed to him, and in one of his letters to his mother he wrote: "While at Krasnoyarsk I wrote some poetry starting with 'In the village of Shushensk, beneath the mountains of Sayansk.' Unfortunately I never got beyond the first stanza." What was so unfortunate about this he failed to say.[2]

While in Siberia, Lenin married a fellow intellectual, Nadezhda Krupskaya, whom he had met romantically in St. Petersburg when she was distributing his leaflets to factory workers. It is true that he despised legal marriage. But, we are told, he "went through the motions" with Nadezhda, both of them apparently keeping their fingers crossed throughout the ceremony. They spent their honeymoon translating Sidney and

---

[1] He grew quite adept at skimming the ice off a bottle of ink.

[2] If the reader will try to find rhymes for Shushensk and Sayansk, he will appreciate the problems of Russian poets.

Beatrice Webb's *Theory and Practice of Trade Unionism.*[1] In a tender mood they made longhand copies of Lenin's *Development of Capitalism in Russia* by moonlight. Sometimes they were alone briefly, but before you could say Krzhizhanovskaya they would be joined by a merry throng of political exiles, clamoring for Lenin to tell them his hilarious dialect story about the two bourgeoisie. For an encore he would give them something full of thrills and suspense, perhaps a statistical report on working conditions in Minsk, and everyone would be as quiet as a mousk.

The life of the Party

A PUBLISHING VENTURE

Released from Sibera, Lenin made his way to Germany, where he published a revolutionary paper called *Iskra.*[2] It was printed on onionskin paper, good for smuggling into Russia where it could be used for making onion soup after being read. After a time, however, the printer in Munich refused to continue. This sensitive man was unable to take it, day after day,

[1] Written, we assume, by Sidney and Beatrice on *their* honeymoon.
[2] Which is "Arksi" spelled backward.

37

watching his typesetters weep over their presses. So Lenin headed for London, muttering imprecations against German sentimentality.

IN LONDON

In London, Lenin bought a street map and soon learned where he could find the most ugliness and poverty.[1] He loved to depress himself by a good walk through the slums. Often he would engage in conversation with some sodden character, urging him to throw off his chains and unite with the workers

A good walk through the slums

of the world. But when the poor fellow insisted that work was the last bloody thing he wanted and asked for tuppence to buy a spot of bitters, Lenin would stalk angrily away. This sort of thing was bad for the revolution.

Mostly he sat in the library of the British Museum, reading Marx, perhaps in the very seat where Marx had read Hegel and where later generations of intellectuals were to read Lenin.

[1] At night he read himself to sleep over Gorky's *Lower Depths*.

38

Had the bourgeoisie removed the chairs from the library of the British Museum, they might long since have put an end to Communism.

But Lenin, clutching a forged library card, read on and on, leaving his fingerprints on the margins of history.

FURTHER TRAVELS

The offices of *Iskra* were now moved to Switzerland, and Lenin went with them, stubbornly remaining at his desk. At this time Lenin was one of the leaders of the Social Democrats —a group cleverly named, since they were neither. However they did attempt to pep up their dismal meetings with games and amusements, such as Pin-the-Tail-on-the-Banker and Cut-the-Head-off-the-Capitalist, and therefore became known as "the Party." But a split ensued between the Mensheviks and the Boysheviks, led by Lenin. (The word Boysheviks was soon corrupted to Bolsheviks, and we shall henceforth use the latter, having a fondness for the corrupt.) Sharp differences of opinion arose. For instance the Bolsheviks wanted to hang capitalists from every lamppost, while the more moderate Mensheviks proposed hanging them from every other lamppost.

Lenin was forever crossing off the days and weeks on his calendar, growing increasingly impatient for the Revolution of 1917. In 1905 he went back to Russia and took part in a small-sized dress rehearsal.[1] After working the Bolsheviks into a frenzy with his speeches, in which he urged them to shoot, stab, or burn, he left for Finland. From there he was able to watch the rise and fall of the armed revolt with a certain detachment.

After this abortive revolution, Lenin needed to raise funds for the Party. For some reason wealthy people seemed unwilling to donate, even when promised a sticker for their window saying "We Gave." Being a very practical man, Lenin solved the problem by printing his own money,[2] and further augmented his income by supervising the robbing of banks. He

---

[1] There was no admission charge, and the performers were very nervous.

[2] He had a green thumb for this sort of thing, or from it.

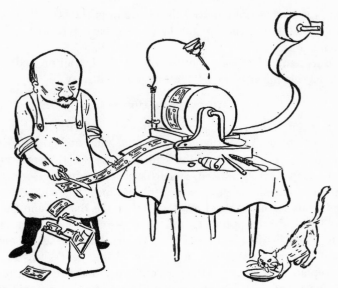

A practical financier

would see his fund raisers off every morning, urging them to mangle or strangle anyone who stood in their way.[1] Then he would turn back to the solicitous letter he was writing to his mother, whose tendency to catch cold worried him.

In 1912 the Bolsheviks began publishing a newspaper in St. Petersburg called *Pravda*,[2] and Lenin was the unofficial editor. However, he stayed in Cracow, across the border, since the sound of whirring presses and the smell of printer's ink made him giddy.

AT THE OUTBREAK OF WORLD WAR I

When World War I broke out, Lenin was delighted to think that the flower of Russia, France, Germany, Austria, and England would be destroyed. For all he cared, soldiers could go into

[1] They were not encouraged to be polite toward those ahead of them in the line at the teller's window.

[2] The Russian word for "truth," and you will have to take their word for it.

Holland too, and trample down the tulips. From a vantage point in Switzerland he shouted encouraging slogans to both sides, such as "Turn your guns on your officers!" and "Shoot him in the wallet!" He showed absolutely no fear of shot, shell, or strained vocal cords.

At this time Lenin, who was in his mid-forties, is described as having high cheekbones, intense eyes, a bald head, and a pointed beard (or, in some translations, bold eyes and a pointed head). He had a brief affair with a certain Madame K., but dropped her when he discovered that she had never read *Das Kapital*. "I have yet to meet a woman," Lenin is quoted as saying, "who can do these three things: understand Marx, play chess, and read a railroad timetable." But he kept searching, mostly in libraries and railway stations, with a chess set under his arm.

REVOLUTION AT LAST

Lenin was in Switzerland, expecting an uprising in Italy and keeping hopefully in touch with England, when the Revolution of 1917 took place in Russia. The Czar was ousted and the

Revolution at last

41

Soviet government took over. This was the sort of thing Lenin had been dreaming of for years, and here he was hemmed in by Alpine scenery, unable to see that long-awaited massacre of the nobility. He was suddenly sick of Swiss cheese and edelweiss. He wanted to get to Russia the worst way.

This turned out to be a sealed train, Lenin being too large for a sealed envelope. On this Famous Ride across Germany, then at war with Russia, Lenin was kept from getting off to buy a newspaper or give a speech. It was probably the stuffiest trip in the history of the steam engine.

Lenin's train arrived on time [1] at the Finland station, which naturally is not in Finland but in Russia. Lenin had not set foot on the soil of his homeland in ten years, and, since he was at once hoisted onto the shoulders of the enthusiastic crowd awaiting him, it appeared he would have to wait a little longer. His arrival, historians tell us, spelled doom (d-o-o-m) for the monarchy.

STRUGGLE FOR POWER

Then followed an exciting time of revolution, counterrevolution, and counter-counterrevolution. The Provisional Government, under Kerensky, had more provisions, but the Bolsheviks, under Lenin, had a superior supply of slogans. Day after day he worked bravely at his desk. In the small hours of the morning (during which he worked under greater pressure than in the large hours of the afternoon) he would come forth with some such battle cry as "The time is now!" or, in a moment of inspiration, "Now is the time!"

These he would hand to a messenger, to be carried posthaste to Bolshevik Party Headquarters. There the Central Committee, who met around the clock,[2] would fall upon each slogan with breathless admiration and commit it to memory.

Eventually, however, Kerensky got the upper hand and Lenin was forced to flee to Finland.[3] He traveled Incognito,

[1] That is, in 1917.

[2] Set in the center of the table.

[3] Where he arrived, we presume, at the Russian station.

which cost a little more than Third Class but was worth the difference. In Finland he stayed for several days in a haystack, which was very nearly the last straw.

From Finland, Lenin kept sending messages and slogans to Bolshevik leaders in Russia, urging them to lay down their lives for the Revolution. At first they were unenthusiastic. But on November 7, 1917,[1] the Bolsheviks seized the government and, instead of banishing Kerensky to Siberia, sent him off on a lecture tour to the United States. Lenin then rose to power on a wave of revolting peasants. The tide was running strong.

LENIN TAKES OVER

As head of the new government, Lenin lost no time publishing decrees and issuing Fiats.[2] He speedily established what he called a dictatorship of the proletariat. "Every man a dictator" was his finest slogan,[3] though he reserved for himself the right to be the dictators' dictator.

Lenin's first step was to take over the State Bank. As its

[1] Called the October Revolution by someone who had forgotten to change his calendar.

[2] This was long before Hitler began manufacturing the Volkswagen.

[3] His second finest was "A capitalist in every pot."

43

director he appointed Vladimir Kopek, a Bolshevik with unusual banking experience: for many years he had had a small checking account. As assistant director he named Ivan Balpointski, a man who had made his mark, being unable to sign his name. Gone were the days when the Bolsheviks had to hold up armored trucks to obtain funds for the Party.

The next step was to close down all the newspapers, since Lenin felt that the Russian people were wasting valuable man-hours puzzling over the truth. A few papers, such as *Pravda* and *Izvestia,* were permitted to resume publication in order that the full text of Lenin's speeches could be printed for public consumption.

Finally, Lenin established the Extraordinary Commission for Combating Counterrevolution and Speculation, known by those who didn't want to take all day about it as Cheka. Its members were the secret police, later called OGPU, NKVD, MVD, and PSST! Lenin got so he preferred Chekas to chess. He ordered them to shoot at sight, or even at sound, anyone plotting against the government. He had only to nod his head and Dzerzhinsky, the chief of Cheka, would start scratching his itchy trigger finger. Once Lenin grew drowsy at a meeting of Commissars when Dzerzhinsky was present, and it cost the lives of several hundred political prisoners.

IN THE KREMLIN

Lenin, who had come to power in St. Petersburg,[1] soon moved to Moscow and took up residence in the Kremlin, a building full of secret passages, secret police, drafty halls, and the sweet smell of arsenic. He immediately felt at home. In his office he kept a blackboard where he could readily post the latest figures on the number of bourgeoisie removed from (1) office, (2) Russia, (3) this mortal coil. Despite the strain of work and responsibility, Lenin remained remarkably good-humored. Report of a particularly clever piece of sabotage would keep him in high spirits for an entire day.

He maintained stern discipline. At meetings of the People's

[1] Or Petrograd. Later Leningrad. Some day Khrushchevgrad?

Lenin in high spirits

Commissars, over which Lenin presided, smoking was forbidden. There was always the possibility of bombs under the table.

Lenin's wife was now People's Vice-Commissar of Education, in charge of the propagation of vice in the public schools.[1] Lenin treated her like any other civil servant. "I can always have you shot," he reminded her when she forgot to shine his boots or interrupted while he was talking. In their more tender moments he called her "Comrade, baby."

CIVIL WAR

It must not be supposed that all Russians eagerly accepted Lenin as their leader. Among those who were unenthusiastic were the Cossacks, the Right Social Revolutionaries, the Wrong Social Revolutionaries, terrorists who thought him not terrible enough, splinter groups (some of whom had gone all to pieces), Army officers, and several million starving peasants. These stubborn people waged a Civil War against the Bolsheviks for almost three years. One Social Revolutionary, a woman named

---

[1] Though no optimist, Lenin was a nepotist.

Dora Kaplan, "succeeded in lodging a bullet in the spine of Lenin." Lodgings for bullets were at a premium, so many backs already being occupied.

The conflict seesawed (and teeter-tottered) across Russia. In the north a threat was posed by troops under a quarrelsome general by the name of Wrangel. To the west there was opposition from Poland, and first Pilsudski was thrown back across the Bug and then the Bug was thrown back across Pilsudski. On still another front enemy forces were repelled by Trotsky, who was repelling when he wasn't revolting.

Finally the opponents of the Bolsheviks were routed, most of them to the United States and other capitalist countries. Grand dukes became headwaiters.[1] Grand duchesses became nursemaids.[2] Counts and countesses gave language lessons, teaching movie stars how to pronounce English with a Russian accent. Some worked as porters but tired of it and became exporters. Many went into vodka or caviar, in the latter in-

[1] With the unhappy result that headwaiters have been acting like grand dukes ever since.

[2] Mostly they nursed grudges.

White Russians

stance up to their elbows. Dressed in coats with moth-eaten fur collars, these proud *émigrés* gathered in dimly lit Russian restaurants to listen to the strumming of balalaikas, drink toasts to the Czar, and compare notes about openings for doormen. As the years went by, they gradually went pale with longing for the Good Old Days and became known as White Russians.

DREAMS OF WORLD REVOLUTION

Not satisfied with taking over Russia, Lenin dreamed of a great revolution that would spread Communism all over the world. He coveted for everyone the right to be purged without trial or prescription.

To this end he developed the Communist International, or Comintern.[1] With this he hoped to overthrow the bourgeois governments of neighboring countries, in what came to be known as his Bad Neighbor Policy. He hoped to achieve the result with bloodshed, but was willing to do it peacefully if all other means failed.

[1] The Communists liked to shorten things, for instance the life span of capitalists.

CHAPTER IV

RUSSIA UNDER LENIN

A NEW DAY was dawning, and the tsars were dimming in the
east. Difficulties might lie ahead, but only during a brief transi-
tional period. Everyone happily tightened his belt, or put on
suspenders.[1]

In the new government, the working class was the base.
This situation was readily accepted by the Russian peasants,
who had had centuries of experience in starting at the bottom
and remaining there. They had nothing to lose, they were told,
but their chains,[2] and they were ready to make the sacrifice.

---

[1] Peasants who had neither were in for some embarrassing moments.
[2] No mention being made of their lives.

If a shot was occasionally heard in the distance, it was probably someone who was merely discharging his debt to society.

THE VOTING SYSTEM

It has been rumored that Lenin's government provided no opportunity for the common man to vote. Nothing could be further from the truth. The Russian worker was kept so busy voting that production in factories and on farms was seriously affected.

The reason for so much voting was that each village elected a village soviet which elected a canton soviet which elected a district soviet which elected a national soviet which elected a large committee which elected a small central committee which elected a chairman who, since he didn't believe in God, refused to let things go any farther.

Voting was by a show of hands and had to be at least unanimous. Anyone refusing to show his hands was suspected of having dirty fingernails. This made it easy to see who voted for whom and simplified the work of the secret police, who were always on the lookout for Deviationists, Tangentialists, and Peripheralists.

While peasants and workers had their hands up, Commissars were given a splendid opportunity to pick their pockets, which, alas, were usually empty.

The Russian peasant at the bottom . . .

Voting was by a show of hands

FUNCTION OF THE PARTY

Under Lenin, the name of the Bolshevik Party was changed to the Communist Party. The Party started at the grass roots, with members who preferred to remain underground, and went up to the All-Russian Congress, in which every Congressman was 100 per cent Russian. In actual control of the organization were what are referred to as "several small bodies," probably dwarfs, named Politburo and Orgburo. Even more frightening was Rabkrin, which "had wide powers to examine office archives and watch administrators at work." An administrator, after being watched by Rabkrin for a few weeks, usually put his head on his desk and sobbed uncontrollably.[1]

At first the Government and the Communist Party were separate, except for the fact that you had to be a member of the Party to get into the Government. Eventually the Party discouraged competition by outlawing all parties except

[1] Out of consideration for readers with a high pulse rate, no mention will be made of the even more terrifying Sovnarkom and Glavkomtrud.

itself for the sake of clarity, simplicity, and the Communist Party. This drastically reduced the number of 100-rubles-a-plate dinners, which in turn meant fewer after-dinner speakers, stale jokes about capitalists, and vodka hang-overs.[1]

Rabkrin watching an administrator

LIFE IN THE FACTORY

There was an impressive change in the life of factory workers. For one thing, they formed themselves into committees and spent most of their time making motions. These were usually with fists clenched, in the direction of the management. Skilled workers got so they could operate a drill press with one hand and take notes with the other. Industrial production fell off, but there was a boom in the Russian edition of *Robert's Rules of Order*.

Behind every worker stood a Commissar, handing him his hammer, sickle, and screwdriver. On request he would read funny stories by Groucho, Harpo, and Karlo Marx. One of

[1] Thanks to the Cheka, however, cases of nervous indigestion were on the increase.

A Commissar behind every worker

the most hilarious—now being made into a musical comedy—begins like this: "The rate of surplus value, or the degree of exploitation of labor-power, and the value of labor-power, or the amount of necessary time being given, it is self-evident that the greater the variable capital, the greater would be the mass value time produced and of the surplus-value." It sustains this excruciating level to the end, which is a long way off.

Behind every Commissar, of course, was another Commissar, and behind that Commissar still another Commissar, all the way from the factory to the Kremlin. The farther back a Commissar was, the higher his rank, which meant that a Commissar got ahead by getting behind. Now and then a visiting peasant would try to edge into line, thinking everyone must be queued up for a bowl of borsch. Until his death, Lenin was the last man in the line, a situation which was reversed when crowds came to see how he was making out in his tomb.

LIFE ON THE FARM

In farming areas, meanwhile, an even more significant change was being instituted. Under the Czars, Russian farmers had been of only two classes: Industrious and Lazy. But Lenin, who was thought to believe in a classless society, slyly divided them into three classes in order to confuse his critics.[1] These were the poor peasant, or *bednyak,* the middle-class peasant, or *double-bednyak,* and the upper-class peasant, or *kulak,* who affected high-toned manners, such as stirring his tea with his little finger crooked.

Lenin's objective was to get the three classes of peasants so busy fighting each other that they wouldn't notice when his agents, disguised as tractors,[2] carried off the newly harvested

Bednyak and kulak

crops. It remained for Stalin, however, to solve the farm problem by plowing under the *kulaks,* thereby reducing the number of mouths to feed and enriching the impoverished soil.

LIFE IN THE HOME

Free love, despite centuries of practice (see Rasputin, above), was not yet perfect. In the early years of Communism, however, advances were made by both sexes. Since his disillusionment with Madame K., Lenin had given the country

[1] Or possibly to invite comparison with Julius Caesar and what he did with Gaul.
[2] With muffled treads.

little leadership in this regard, but some of his young lieu-tenants, such as Lt. Ataman Oboy and Lt. Igor Kumonsky (known as Igor the Vigorous), tried to keep interest alive.

Braving disapproval by the Party, many old-fashioned Rus-sians still managed to marry. Wedding rings could be obtained on the black market, and the wedding ceremony could always be disguised as a workers' meeting. Relatives of the groom were posted outside to give warning of a raid, and in an emergency everyone could swing into the *"Internationale."*

It was part of the Marxist ideology that "the family is a bourgeois crutch." This probably goes back to the fact that Marx hoped his six children would eventually support him. The trouble with family life was that people got attached to each other and wanted to stay home nights instead of going out to hear lectures on subjects such as "Materialism and Empirio-Criticism" and "A Comparison of the Output of Pig Iron in Central Europe and in East Asia."

An exciting alternative to bourgeois life in the home was Communist life in the barracks, with everyone sharing alike—the same roof, the same floor, and the same towel. A single siren at 5 A.M. saved precious time spent winding and setting hundreds of alarm clocks. Common meals eliminated invidi-ous comparisons and heightened the feeling of Togetherness.

THE DEATH OF LENIN

If we have several times anticipated the death of Lenin, it should be ascribed not to faulty organization but to impatience. He died as a comparatively young man, in 1924, having "burnt himself out," perhaps as a result of friction from rubbing peo-ple the wrong way. An autopsy revealed that his brain had shrunk to about one-quarter of normal size, although Profes-sor Rozanov, who reported this condition, failed to state whether this happened during Lenin's fatal illness or in his youth.

Lenin's body was embalmed and placed in a glass case in

Red Square, where it may be viewed even today.[1] Russians and visitors from all over the world queue up to get a good look and to praise the embalmer, who has been raised to the rank of Folk Hero. Little did Lenin think he would end up as a Tourist Attraction.

[1] Lenin had always wanted to make Russia a showcase of Communism, and it was fitting that he should become Exhibit A. For Exhibit B, see the end of the chapter on Stalin, below.

CHAPTER V

TROTSKY

THE NAMES of Lenin and Trotsky are popularly linked, much like those of Marx and Engels, Damon and Pythias, and Chesapeake and Ohio. These two Communist leaders saw eye to eye, both being on the short side and shortsighted.

Trotsky was the oddest looking of the top Communists, a strange little man with a pince-nez and a shock of black hair that stood on end as if his finger were in a light socket.[1] Indeed we have read that on one occasion, when he suddenly arrived at a Party caucus, "his appearance was electrifying."

[1] Unlike Lenin, Trotsky kept his hair. Of course Lenin may also have kept his, placing it hair by hair in a box on his dressing table.

Trotsky, who was ten years younger than Lenin, had all the qualifications of a revolutionary leader. To wit:

1. He was born with a name, Lev Davydovich Bronstein, which could easily be changed to Trotsky.

2. He was expelled from school. It seems he led a demonstration against his French teacher, when she complained about his filching snails from her lunch box. The other pupils wanted him to demonstrate.

3. He spent the requisite number of years in prison and in exile.

4. He married a fellow intellectual, six years older than himself, irresistibly attracted by her high forehead and her low shoes. Employing the Marxian dialectic, he won her by insisting that two can discuss socialist philosophy better than one.

BACKGROUND AND CHARACTER

From the outset, Trotsky felt himself a cut above his fellow revolutionaries. His father, although a peasant, was a well-to-do peasant who could afford little luxuries, such as an extra manure pile. It is true that this was the very type later liquidated by the Communists. But there is no use haggling over fine points.

There was something aloof and aristocratic in Trotsky's manner which ideally fitted him to be a champion of the common man. This coolness in his personality was doubtless a result of his long exile in the arctic. One of his contemporaries comments on his "complete lack of charm," a quality especially noticeable when he was purging old friends. Another refers to his "acid tongue." This must have caused him no little discomfort and may explain his irritability.

Little Lev was something of a prodigy. At six months he was taking quick mincing steps. "Look, he's trotskying!" exclaimed his mother, making her contribution to history. At five he caused a family crisis by explaining the facts of life to his twelve-year-old brother. At seven he could speak three languages, which was not so remarkable except that he could

Champion of the common man

speak all three at once. It was evident that the lad would be heard from.

CAREER OF REVOLUTION

Trotsky fell in with a group of radicals and by eighteen was printing illegal leaflets. These he circulated among factory workers, thus starting the first on-the-job training program.

He had found his calling. With Marx and Lenin he would go down in history as one of The Three Pamphleteers, marching arm in arm and chanting the old Nihilist motto: "None for all and all for none."

Eventually, however, he was caught and thrown into prison. There he married a fellow political prisoner, a Marxist named Alexandra Sokolovskaya. It was a romantic instance of cell mates becoming soul mates.

In prisons in Nikolayev, Odessa, and Moscow, Trotsky discovered a hidden talent, that of writing the words and music of revolutionary songs. One of his earliest compositions, full of the tenderness and compassion for which his ditties came to be famous, is "Katchuska," written while he was recovering from an attack of sneezing brought on by the prison's dampness. The first stanza, reprinted here by permission of the copyright holders, Lev, Davydovich, and Bronstein Music Corp., goes as follows:

> *Comrades, now the world is yours,*
> *Gently flow its open sewers.*
> *If a corpse goes floating by,*
> *Yours is not to reason why.*[1]
> *If you do, much though we sorrow,*
> *You'll be in there, too, tomorrow.*

After two years, the door of Trotsky's cell was flung wide. His jailers were music lovers and could take it no longer.[2] He was exiled to Siberia, where he would be out of hearing.

In Siberia, Trotsky and his wife settled in the village of Ust-Kut, attracted by its euphonious name. It was a Godforsaken place, which increased its appeal for atheists. Soon Trotsky was

[1] Trotsky's debt to Tennyson went unacknowledged, as did his debts to his tailor, his butcher, and the corner drugstore.

[2] As he sang, his wife accompanied him by beating on the bars, eight beats to the bar.

Discovered a hidden talent

lecturing anyone who would sit with him on a snowbank, argu-
ing in favor of a rise in wages, living standards, and temperature. This was known as a caucus in the Caucasus. He also
wrote for the Irkutsk paper, the *Nihilist News*. Wielding a pen
helped his circulation, if not that of the paper.

MEETING WITH LENIN

In the summer of 1902, when he was twenty-three, the underground mail brought Trotsky a copy of one of Lenin's books. It
was slow arriving, having been misrouted through a gopher
hole. The book was entitled *What Is to Be Done?* Since
Trotsky knew the answer, he must get to Lenin and tell him. So
he escaped under a cartload of hay, leaving a dummy in his bed.
No one got wise to this for several days, though his guards
thought it strange that Trotsky was leaving so much food on
his plate.

Meanwhile the cart with its load of hay and Trotsky, who
was engrossed in the *Iliad,* rumbled across Siberia toward freedom and better reading conditions. He arrived in London at
dawn and immediately called on Lenin, with complete disregard
for Visiting Hours. "The door was opened by Nadezhda Kon-
stantinovna, who had probably been wakened by my knock-
ing," says Trotsky in his autobiography, exhibiting his usual
logic and discernment. Trembling with anticipation, he was
escorted into Lenin's bedroom.

It was a Great Meeting of Two Giants of Our Times, a
fabled encounter in the annals of Communism. What matter if
the giants were both barely five feet six? What matter if
Trotsky was still slightly green from a rough Channel crossing,
while Lenin, in a frayed dressing gown, was unable to suppress
an occasional yawn?

The two world-shaking revolutionaries came together and
shared their dreams. "Let me tell you about a dream I had last
night," Lenin and Trotsky blurted out simultaneously. Both
being superstitious, they hooked their little fingers together and
made a wish. What they discussed, as dawn turned to day, we
can only conjecture, but we are told by Trotsky's biographer

that "they talked for hours over a pot of coffee," probably warming themselves in the steam.

Lenin was quite taken by young Trotsky, and in a letter to one of his confederates described him as "a man of conviction and energy, who will go much farther." How much farther he went was a surprise even to Lenin. In subsequent years he was again exiled to Siberia, again escaped,[1] and popped up in

A world-shaking encounter

Vienna, Berlin, Zurich, Helsinki, Belgrade, Paris, Madrid, Cadiz, and the Bronx. Along about 1916 if you were sitting in a café in any of the capitals of the world and saw a little man at the next table with a shock of black hair, thick glasses, and a mustache and goatee, the chances are it wasn't Trotsky.

While changing places, Trotsky also changed names, his passports being issued to Arbuzov, Yanovsky, Vikentiev, Samokovlieff, and so on. He also changed wives, from Alexandra Sokolovskaya to Natalya Sedova, though he carelessly neglected to divorce the first one, which may explain why he kept on the move. Because he was a true revolutionary, the one thing he seldom changed was his shirt.

[1] This time, to confuse the authorities, he and the dummy escaped together.

HIS PART IN THE REVOLUTION

Trotsky was not always an admirer of Lenin, unless some of his writings during the Bolshevik-Menshevik feud, when he referred to Lenin as "hideous," "dissolute," "demagogical," "slovenly," and "malicious and morally repulsive," have suffered in translation. Later he saw which side of his toast the caviar was on.

In 1917, when the Revolution broke out, Trotsky was in New York. There he experienced the pleasures and pains of capitalism. When he lunched at upper-class restaurants such as the Automat, he hated himself for it, and got a modicum of satisfaction when he sprung a piece of pie with a copper kopek.[1] For a time Trotsky worked as a dishwasher, enraged at how much these capitalists left on their plates. At night, in his Bronx apartment, he whipped up the revolutionary fervor of his friends by showing them his dishpan hands.

[1] Then worth approximately two and one-half bottle tops.

A dishwasher's frustration

62

When the call came (collect), Trotsky got to Petrograd as fast as he could. Since not even one-tenth of one per cent of the population were Bolsheviks, Lenin needed an orator like Trotsky to persuade the Russians that this was the party of the majority. Because Trotsky had been away from Russia so long, Lenin thought of calling him his Foreign Commissar. Later he made him Commissar for War, well knowing that if anyone was for war it was Trotsky.

Trotsky's greatest contribution was as the mobilizer of a huge army. A tireless speaker,[1] he loved to emerge suddenly from the muzzle of a cannon and make a fiery recruiting speech, urging young Russians to join the Army and see Russia.

While on recruiting tours, Trotsky dramatized his militarism by living in an armored train. Though not sealed like Lenin's, it was equipped with all the comforts of home, such as wheel-to-wheel carpeting and a garbage can for disposal of speeches that went sour.

Despite his lack of military training,[2] Trotsky's tactics made all the generals look sick, especially when he ordered them into the front lines. At the close of World War I, the Soviet armies were fighting on six fronts, and Trotsky somehow managed to be everywhere at once, herding the stragglers before him and shouting, "Courage, boys. Comrade Trotsky is leading you behind!"

Trotsky is known as "the Father of the Red Army." Since history records that he sired only two or three sons, there is obviously more to be known about this indefatigable campaigner.

STRUGGLE WITH STALIN

After Lenin's death, Trotsky and Stalin became rivals for power. Except for their fondness for aliases, the two men were utterly incompatible, Trotsky a high-strung, talkative intellectual and Stalin a stolid, quiet peasant. Stalin's technique was to let Trotsky talk, hoping he would put his foot in his mouth

---

[1] His audiences had a good deal of endurance too.

[2] There was no R.O.T.C. unit at the University of Odessa.

and choke to death. Their struggle was waged in many odd ways. Once, at a meeting in the Kremlin, Trotsky denounced Stalin in a fiery speech and then made a dramatic exit, slamming the door behind him. Appearing from nowhere, Stalin stuck his fingers in the door so that it would close noiselessly, thus ruining Trotsky's exit.[1]

Trotsky advocated world Communism, while Stalin favored concentrating on Russia. Unlike Trotsky, who had spent the best years of his life abroad,[2] Stalin was a home-town boy with a narrow outlook.[3] Large though it was, Russia wasn't big enough for the two of them.

When Lenin died, Trotsky was on vacation in the Caucasus, resting his vocal cords. On his return to Moscow he found himself ousted from his position as Commissar for War and assigned to a small post connected with the development of electric power.[4] He started on an inspection tour of electric stations, but it was a short circuit. Stalin banished him from Russia.

[1] And Stalin's hand.

[2] Which is why they were the best years.

[3] Next time you look at a picture of Stalin, notice his close-set eyes.

[4] See what happened to Malenkov, below. Under the Communist system a Party leader is often downgraded from political power to electric.

64

Trotsky went to Mexico by way of Turkestan, Constantinople, and Norway, either hoping to elude pursuers or misrouted by an inexperienced clerk in a travel bureau. In Mexico he settled in a pleasant villa in Coyoacán, a suburb of Mexico City. There, idyllically surrounded by high concrete walls and machine-gun towers, he continued his work as the number one Trotskyite, day after day thumbing a thesaurus for suitable invectives to apply to the Stalinists.

On August 20, 1940, Trotsky was assassinated by a young man who said he was an admirer who had come to pick his brains, and proceeded to do so with a pickax. Although Stalin blamed the murder on a Mexican who was hopped up by tequila and full of jumping beans, it is noteworthy that he sent no flowers.

TROTSKY'S CONTRIBUTION

Trotsky is one of the major historians of Communism, among other things having written a biography of Lenin and a book called *My Life,* in which he was unable to avoid an occasional favorable reference to himself. He was at work on a somewhat critical biography of Stalin when he was interrupted by the visitor with the pickax. The manuscript, which had been full of spleen, was now full of cerebellum as well.[1]

Trotsky is remembered for advocating "permanent revolution," wishing to keep revolutionists like himself constantly employed. Some believe that he was a purer Marxist than Stalin, and that, had he succeeded Lenin, things would have been different. They would have, for Trotsky.

[1] See Trotsky's earlier work on Stalin as an educator, *The Stalin School of Falsification.* The reader who wishes something lighter may enjoy his *Defense of Terrorism.*

CHAPTER VI

THE RISE OF STALIN

IN VIEW OF his bloody career, it is appropriate that Stalin was born, on December 21, 1879, in a place called Gori. This "rock-strewn town"[1] was situated in Georgia, fifty miles west of Tiflis and no telling how far east of Atlanta.

Stalin, born Joseph Vissarionovich Djugashvili, was affection-ately called "Soso" by his mother, who frankly thought him only average. Following the precedent set by Lenin and Trot-sky, he replaced Djugashvili with Stalin, meaning "steel."

[1] An ideal place for a boy with a slingshot.

However, not even his closest friends ever referred to him as Stainless Stalin.[1]

As a boy, Stalin worked for his father, a shoemaker, and early showed a fondness for leaving nails sticking up inside shoes. He enjoyed watching customers limp out of the shop. During his apprenticeship he learned some of the shrewd aphorisms which later gave color to his writings and speeches, such as "Why try to lift yourself by your bootstraps when I would be glad to do it with a rope?"

But his mother decided on another way her son might save men's soles. She sent him first to a religious preparatory school and then to the seminary in Tiflis. When Soso petitioned to take a reading course in Advanced Atheism, claiming to have all the prerequisites, the authorities began to wonder about his call to the cloth.

Although he stayed on for five years, to please his mother, he was secretly a member of the revolutionary underground. During the day a student of theology, at night he sneaked into town and consorted with a gang of delinquents who had evil designs on their Sunday-school teacher. His double life was discovered when he was found in the library with a Bible on the table and a copy of *Das Kapital* in his lap, and he was expelled. His mother maintains that she took him home for his health. In view of the disfavor he was in with the school authorities, this may simply be a matter of interpretation.

HE BECOMES A FULL-TIME REVOLUTIONIST

Fresh from the seminary, Stalin took up revolution as a career and joined the Bolsheviks. They thrust him into a responsible position at once, appointing him treasurer of the local branch. His duty was to rob a bank the first of each month, when there were bills to pay. His biggest armed robbery

---

[1] According to Trotsky, Stalin eventually used seventeen different names, which made it hard to keep his account straight at the bank. One of them, Ryaboi, or "pock-marked," was given him by the police and was seldom heard after he became a power in the Party.

was in Tiflis in 1907, when he and the assistant treasurer shot up the town and brought a touch of the Far West to the Near East. Stalin's only advance over the technique of Jesse James was his trick of rolling bombs down the main street, which had a way of thinning out traffic and clearing a parking place in front of the bank. He became known as "the Georgian bandit," because his mustache drooped at the ends and he affected a drawl.

People who came up against Stalin in those early days felt something cold about him, probably the muzzle of his revolver.

The Party treasurer at work

He was emotionless and quiet—a man of few words, none of them pleasant. There was a flinty look in his eyes, and an almost imperceptible smile played around his lips.[1] With his low forehead, uncombed hair, and unshaven face, he looked like a thug. His looks were not deceiving.

HUNTED BY THE POLICE

Stalin's activities were becoming known to the Czar, whose secret police could no longer keep the secret. The Czar hated

[1] When tired of playing, it ducked under his mustache.

the thought of revolution and tried to think of something more pleasant, such as the Czarina's new chambermaid. But too many banks were being robbed, too many trains derailed. He ordered the police to tighten their net. They did, and to their surprise Stalin was in it, cleverly disguised as a butterfly.

No one knows how many times Stalin was arrested and imprisoned. Sometimes he stayed in for the full sentence, so busy haranguing prisoners and inciting mess hall revolts,[1] that his term was up before he knew it. Any time he wanted to escape, however, he had only to pull some little trick on his jailer, for instance asking if he might jingle his key ring. He resolved that when he got into power the old easygoing [2] way of prison life would stop.

At the height of his revolutionary activity it is said that Stalin, hunted by the Czarist police, "slept every night in a different house." This accounts for the fact that in subsequent years Stalin Slept Here signs could be seen throughout all of Russia.

EXILE

Between 1903 and 1913 Stalin was exiled to Siberia six times, establishing a record never since equaled. They laughed, that first time at the Tiflis railway station when he insisted on a round-trip ticket, but after two or three trips issued it without question. He had several ingenious ways of escaping, one of which was to read aloud from Marx to his guards, slipping out as soon as they fell asleep.

His years spent in Siberia were actually a blessing to Stalin. As one biographer has said about the effects of Siberian exile, "The Czar, intent on the destruction of his enemies, only succeeded in setting them up, physically and mentally." Stalin was free to go hunting and fishing, get plenty of invigorating fresh air, and read volumes of subversive literature, all at government expense. Thus it was that he went to Siberia thin,

[1] Some of which were pretty messy. See the famous Mashed Potato Riots of 1908.

[2] Out the window and over the wall.

tubercular, and behind in his reading, and came back with a fine physique, a flourishing mustache, and the Will to Win. His ability to concentrate while in Siberia gave Stalin the idea for the concentration camps to which he was later to send the philosophers and intellectuals with whom he had a difference of opinion.

Stalin in Siberia

INFLUENCE OF LENIN

Stalin first met Lenin, who was nine years older, when he was twenty-six. Lenin's personal magnetism made itself felt at once, almost pulling the iron buttons off Stalin's blouse. Stalin in turn interested Lenin, who wondered how a man with such a low forehead could wear a hat. They shared a passion for chess and played game after game, Stalin always confident he could win the next one.

It was under Lenin, Stalin has said, that he "mastered the art of revolution," assuming revolution to be an art rather than a craft. Previously Stalin had used such crude tools as the bomb and the revolver, but Lenin opened his eyes to such subtle and

70

Stalin's last move

silent methods as the Big Lie, the Middle-Sized Lie, and the Tiny Fib.[1]

A NARROW ESCAPE

By a curious quirk of history, Stalin narrowly escaped being drafted into the Czar's army in 1916. All that saved him was a tennis elbow [2] which would have impaired his soldierly efficiency at lifting a tankard. The examining physician may also have noticed that two toes on Stalin's left foot were grown together. While this would not have affected his counting on his fingers, it might have led to inaccuracies in his dealing with the higher numbers.

BACK FROM SIBERIA

When the Revolution of 1917 broke out, Stalin was wintering in Siberia. He pulled up stakes (they had him tied down) and headed for Petrograd, where he joined Lenin and Trotsky. Like the latter, he had never worn a uniform, but he was immediately given command of an army, with rank equivalent to that of a

---

[1] Obviously the Reds could not use White lies.
[2] See also, below, his foot fault.

71

full general. Later, having risen this far without Basic Training, he promoted himself to Generalissimo.[1]

Stalin's most famous military pronouncement was in the form of a question: "How many divisions has the Pope?" What the Generalissimo overlooked, when he cast doubts on the Pope's strength, was the toughness of the Swiss Guards, who had trained on Swiss steak. Furthermore, they could always shoot from behind a shield of tourists.

Trained on Swiss steak

MEMBER OF THE POLITBURO

In the Bolshevik government under Lenin, Stalin became one of the five members of the Politburo, a group of courteous gentlemen who were always bowing to each other and trying to summon a smile. As a member of this body, Stalin was entitled to a seat in the reviewing stand and a room with a semiprivate bath in the Kremlin.[2] But Lenin and Trotsky made all the speeches and received all the plaudits, Stalin seeming content

---

[1] Napoleon, Hitler, and Mussolini at least got as far as corporal before they discarded the promotion system.

[2] Because of ubiquitous Commissars, no bath could be considered completely private.

to puff silently on his pipe in the background. He was biding his time. As a time bider, he has no equal in history.

Lenin had been in power only a few years when his health began to fail and he tottered on the brink. Trotsky suggests that Stalin, who hated to see anyone suffer, gave him a nudge.

In his last months, Lenin was increasingly offended by Stalin's table manners, objecting to the way he would reach clear across the table to sprinkle something in his borsch. This is why he wrote in his famous testament [1] that Stalin was "too rude" and should be removed from office. However, Stalin went

Stalin's table manners

right on having his picture taken with Lenin at every opportunity, even when it was necessary to prop him up to make him look alive. It is said that he had to guide Lenin's hand in inscribing the deathbed photo with its "To Stalin—My Buddy."

In 1924 Lenin passed on—whither, it is not within our province to conjecture. It was the moment Stalin had been waiting, hoping, and we almost said praying, for.

COMPLETE POWER

No one expected Stalin to succeed Lenin. After all, Lenin had left the man nothing but a few insults to remember him by. Moreover, there was always Trotsky, a dangerous rival who

[1] Famous everywhere but in Russia, where it was not published until 1956, by which time it seemed a little dated.

had incensed Stalin with his Pan-Russian proposals. Nobody, muttered Stalin, was going to pan Russia and get away with it.

Only those close to him, who noticed the widening gap between his trouser cuffs and his shoes, realized that Stalin was gaining stature. He had been appointed General Secretary of the Party, but instead of taking minutes he was taking hours to record nasty remarks and innuendoes which were later to prove invaluable.

Finally he showed his hand. Before long all of him was in plain view. He wasn't voted into power; he didn't seize power. He simply noticed that Lenin's chair was empty and sat down.[1] Visitors to the Front Office noticed a new picture over Stalin's head, a picture of Stalin, smiling.

[1] His rivals were attending memorial services.

CHAPTER VII

THE STALIN ERA

LENIN HAD DREAMED of electrifying Russia. It was an odd dream, with power lines in a terrifying tangle, sparks leaping out of the ground, and peasants leaping straight into the air. He was always glad when his alarm clock awakened him.

Stalin tried his best to make Lenin's dream come true. His slogan was "Overtake America," [1] and he set his scientists to work verifying the rumored discoveries of Benjamin Franklin. On stormy days, when lightning might be expected, distinguished physicists like Wattovich and Voltsky could be seen

[1] Ominous Note: switch the syllables in Overtake and see what you get.

running into the wind with kites. One scientist, who insisted that wire was sturdier than string, made only the first of a proposed series of experiments.

Frantically Stalin threw more and more scientists into the project, offering Stalin Medals, Stalin Plaques, Stalin Scrolls, and generous benefits for scientists' widows. He coveted for Russia the great achievements of America: neon signs, pinball machines, and electric chairs. Only after World War II, under Russian scientists like Ulrich von Braunsteig, Heinrich Zwingermann, and Ludwig von und zu Liebfraumilch, were noteworthy advances made in this area.

PLANNING AND PRODUCTION

In order to achieve industrial progress, an Institute of Planning was established, and thousands of qualified planners were graduated. There was an increase in the production of production charts, and a rise in graphs. Never before had the manufacture of thumbtacks reached such a point.

To give workers something to shoot at (a privilege hitherto reserved for the secret police), Stalin inaugurated a series of Five-Year Plans. Everyone was given a five-year calendar. Out of the Five-Year Plans came such economic innovations as the eight-day work week and the edible lunchbox.

The Five-Year Plans were a great success, five years coming to an end in precisely five years, just as had been predicted. Such accuracy in forecasting was hailed throughout Russia. Engrossing statistics, for instance the increase in the number of double-yolk eggs produced in Ukrainian villages with under 500 population, were given extensive coverage in *Pravda*.[1]

A boon to production was Stakhanovism, named after Alexei Stakhanov, an eager-beaver miner who reached his 1937 quota in 1935 and got everybody mixed up about what year it was. Using a pneumatic drill, operated by lung power, Stakhanov hacked out coal so fast that rail facilities were overtaxed and he threatened to bury his village in anthracite. He could do a

[1] There being no Comics, readers had to have something to look forward to on Sunday mornings.

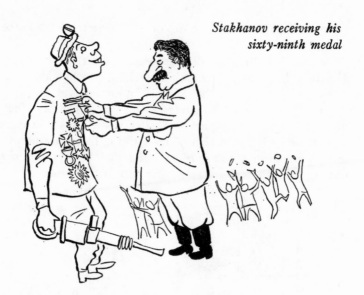

*Stakhanov receiving his
sixty-ninth medal*

day's work in five minutes, and was heartily applauded by Communist Party leaders [1] who stood around with stop watches, ready to make a speech every time a new record was established. Eventually Stakhanov slowed down, sagging under the weight of the sixty-nine Stalin Medals he wore on his blouse.

Coincident with the Five-Year Plan was the Nine-Months' Plan, established to give everyone something to do. This was supervised by the Bureau of Procreation, in whose office were such signs as: "Have You Had a Baby This Year?" and "Cash Prizes for Twins." Young couples were given a Mating Rating and then an all-expense tour to the country, with an opportunity to observe the rabbits. Special awards were given to women who effected a speed-up and produced offspring in seven or eight months. The Mother of the Year, or Mother Russia as she was sometimes called, was widely photographed [2] posing with her children and a production chart. Statistics

[1] And hissed by his fellow workers.
[2] It was necessary to use a wide-angle lens.

being unreliable, no attempt was made to determine the Father of the Year.

To gain time, the State discouraged the folderol of courtship. Usually a boy and girl met while working side by side in the assembly line of, say, the Nizhnii Novgorod Nut and Bolt Works. During their ten minutes off for lunch they blushingly discussed production figures and after a few days exchanged monkey wrenches as a sign of their troth. The State benevolently gave them a change of scene for their honeymoon, permitting them to work in some other part of the factory.

A sign of their troth

HEAVY INDUSTRY

Always Stalin emphasized Heavy Industry. He wanted something that kleptomaniac factory workers couldn't pick up and take home with them. Industry became so heavy, in fact, that floors began to give way at an alarming rate, and it became necessary to build factories underground.

Some difficulty was occasioned by the fact that workers in factories, accustomed to sabotaging production under the Czar, found it hard to break the habit. Often they absent-mindedly slit power belts or threw sand into machinery, and were chagrined when they remembered that the factory belonged to the People.[1] Some of the workers were none too clear about who the People were. Surely it couldn't be they. On second thought, they agreed that they may have been given the works.

INVENTIONS

An outgrowth of industrial progress was a sudden rash of inventions by Russians, many of whom had neglected to take out patents when they first got the idea, forty or fifty years earlier. Among these were the telephone, the radio, the airplane, the safety razor, and the crossword puzzle. There was also the ingenious game of Russian roulette, a boon to self-destruction, which Russians played when they were loaded and hoped the pistol wasn't.

Reference should also be made in passing to that happy invention of V. M. Molotov—the Molotov Cocktail, or Gasoline-on-the-Rocks. To see whether it was strong enough, it was sometimes thrown against the side of a tank. If it exploded in a burst of flames, it was ready for drinking. If not, a little less vermouth was indicated.

AGRICULTURAL DEVELOPMENTS

Agriculture, meanwhile, was undergoing a profound change. This was the result of the *kolkhoz*, or Collective Farm, where peasants worked for everybody instead of themselves and whatever they produced was collected and carted off by the State. Everyone liked the system but the peasants. They were not forced into *kolkhozes*, however, but were given the choice of joining them or starving to death. Most of the *kulaks*, gentlemen farmers who looked suspiciously like capitalists, were carted away [2] by the secret police for questioning. One question never answered was what happened to them.

Peasants who did not wish to give their cows to the State ate them as fast as they could. This led to many deaths from in-

---

[1] A worker with something wrapped around his finger was not wearing a Band-Aid, as might be supposed, but a memory aid.

[2] In their own carts.

digestion, preceded by violent bicarbonate of soda orgies. It was a period of Internal Turbulence.

Mechanization also changed the agricultural picture. Tractors became the most prized possession of the Russian peasant, though owned by the State. They were the subject of many a sentimental ode, such as the beautiful lines by Nikolai Shliapnikov, beginning:

> *I love the way you vibrate, sweet,*
> *I love to feel your bucket seat.*

It was a common occurrence for a farmer to bring his tractor into the bedroom at night and to make his wife sleep in the barn. A woman could be divorced if she came between a man and his tractor. She could also be run over, a harrowing experience.

EMANCIPATION OF WOMEN

It must not be thought, however, that woman's place was always beneath the tractor. During Stalin's dictatorship women were emancipated, which means that they were now permitted to drive trucks, sweep streets, carry ice,[1] fit sewer pipe, and do a hundred and one other things they had always yearned to do. With a few exceptions [2] they could do anything a man could. A new career open to them was the Army, and many learned to shoot a rifle, throw a hand grenade, and go A.W.O.L. Women who had been camp followers now became leaders.

EDUCATION

As for education, there was a rapid rise in literacy. Russian boys and girls became excellent spellers. This was a good thing, because they had to cope with words like Ordjonikidze, Pobedonostsev, Kosmodemyanskaya,[3] and Dnieprodkerzhinsk. To make it easier for Russian school children, histories of Russia were materially shortened by eliminating everything before 1917. They were also published in loose-leaf form to keep up with swiftly changing past events. Interesting facts were being discovered almost daily, for example that Trotsky instead of being a First Class Hero was an enemy of the State.

Similarly, biology textbooks were published with two interchangeable chapters on the work of geneticist T. D. ("Touchdown") Lysenko. One agreed with his theory that the growth of wheat could be stimulated by giving the roots a daily alcohol rub, while the other suspected Lysenko of plotting with the West to make alcoholics of the Russians. Which chapter was used depended on whether Lysenko, who was inclined to be forgetful, had paid his Party dues that month.

On the other hand, there was never any question about the findings of Professor Pavlov, the famous saliva man, who gave dogs schooling in drooling. His greatest scientific achievement was when he got dogs so confused that they imagined they were

[1] This gave rise to a new genre of humor about the icewoman.

[2] For instance they were not permitted, or at least not encouraged, to grow beards.

[3] For those who do not know Russian, the last part of this word, "demyanskaya," means "damn Yankee." For those who do know Russian, it probably means something else.

Women were emancipated

eating dinner whenever they heard a bell ring. Pavlov thus performed an outstanding service to the State by completely eliminating the need for dog food. But for his untimely death, in 1936, he might have done as much for humans.

RELIGION

In the field of religion, Marx and Lenin would have been proud of the achievements of Stalin. Under his leadership there was increased activity by the League of the Godless, the members of which picketed churches with signs reading "Unfair to Organized Atheism" and "Leave the Church in the Lurch." They also placed a copy of *Das Kapital* on the bedside table in every hotel room in Russia, with a suggestion of passages to read when in trouble.[1]

For people who wanted a place to go on Sundays there was the Anti-Religious Museum of Moscow, which featured no sermon and no collection plates. As an old seminary student, Stalin was full of clever ideas for exhibits, including lifelike

[1] It helped to be reading them when seized by the secret police.

wax figures of priests for sticking pins into, and how-to-do-it kits for making Bibles into ash trays. Why Russians continued to sneak off to church, with such a delightful alternative, Stalin could never understand. He also worried about the standard examination on religion required in the schools, which went as follows:

> *Teacher:* What is God?
> *Student:* God is a prejudice of the middle class.
> *Teacher:* Well, you have passed.
> *Student:* Thank God!

Angry because they flunked out of Sunday school

THE PURGE TRIALS

In 1934, Sergei Kirov, a Communist leader in Leningrad, was foully murdered [1] by his secretary's husband, probably because Kirov was working her overtime. Kirov was a good friend of Stalin's and Stalin was incensed. He felt that if his best friends were to be murdered, he should at least be given first refusal. It left him strangely dissatisfied to walk in the funeral procession

---

[1] Those who were murdered fairly never knew how lucky they were.

of a high Party official and realize that he had had no part in his demise.[1]

So he instituted a new type of judicial process known as the Purge Trial, which he tried out on Zinoviev, Kamenev, and other Old Bolsheviks to be sure it would work. If the defendant refused to talk, the prosecutor had only to hold up a bottle and a spoon and the poor fellow would break down completely.

Sometimes Stalin could get what he wanted out of a discredited Bolshevik leader without a purge. There was, for instance, the case of Nikolai Bukharin, whose *A.B.C. of Communism* had established him as an authority on the alphabet. After a few sleepless nights, when he was kept awake by the noise of pistols being cocked, Bukharin confessed everything willingly. Later, having heard the confessions of some of his colleagues, he added a few gruesome episodes in order not to be thought a piker. He was finally carried away by his oratory and by two NKVD men. He had hoped to make the front pages of *Pravda* and *Izvestia*, but disappointingly was given only a brief notice in the obituary column.

The man in charge of these trials was Andrei ("Vicious") Vishinsky, later Foreign Minister and star of the United Nations television spectacular. As professor of criminal law at the University of Moscow he had experimented with various stimulants, such as cold showers and pistol whippings, when students fell asleep in his classes. Stalin gave him the position of Chief Public Prosecutor, and Vishinsky took the title seriously, working overtime at it.

Vishinsky's most memorable words during the Purge Trials were: "I demand that all these mad dogs be shot." Judges, most of them in mortal terror of rabies, acceded to his humanitarian request.

There were often happy reunions when a judge, found dangerous to public health himself, met in the death cell someone

[1] Emil Ludwig quotes Stalin as saying: "The best thing in life is to ferret out one's enemy, prepare the stroke carefully, revenge oneself mercilessly, and then lie down to sleep." He found it exciting, but tiring.

he had sentenced only a few days before. "That's the way the cookie crumbles," say the Russians, who incline toward fatalism.

MINOR DEVELOPMENTS

One minor development was the Communist conception of May Day. On this springtime holiday everyone came to Moscow in a festive mood, eager to view the latest Weapons of Destruction. Breaking with sentimental tradition, those in

May Day

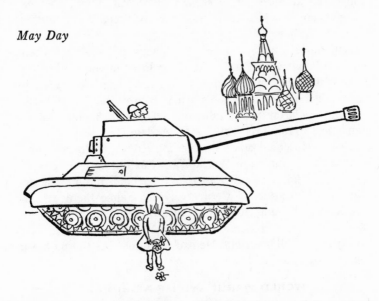

charge requested that flowers be omitted, the money going instead for tanks, planes, and nerve gas.[1]

Another interesting change was the unique way the names of cities were standardized, in the interest of simplicity. Whatever the ending, the first two syllables were the same, as in Stalingrad, Stalinbad, Stalino, Stalinir, Stalinsk, etc. To lend an air of gaiety, large pictures of Stalin were hung at each street

[1] There was no May Queen, either, this being too reminiscent of royalty.

85

corner and draped over the sides of buildings. Statues of Stalin were erected for those who could get the idea better in the round.

THE HITLER-STALIN PACT

The most striking event in international affairs came in 1939, when Stalin signed a nonaggression pact between Soviet Russia and Nazi Germany. It is interesting that Stalin, only two years before, had had thirteen of his closest friends shot because they sought an alliance with Germany. However, though he may have stolen their idea, he at least had the decency not to use it in their lifetime.

A famous photograph of the pact-signing shows Stalin shaking hands with Foreign Minister Joachim von Ribbentrop, each with an inscrutable smile on his face. The ink was hardly dry [1] when Hitler hurled his armies across the Soviet border without declaring war. Stalin was chagrined, having had the same plan in mind for a slightly later date.

Before Hitler's dastardly move into Russia, Stalin had interpreted the beginning of World War II as follows: "It was not Germany who attacked France and England, but France and England who attacked Germany." [2] Of course there was the possibility, he admitted after receiving large shipments of tanks, trucks, and Spam from the Allies, that he had been guilty of a small oversight. He had forgotten that Germany was on Daylight Saving Time.

WORLD WAR II AND ITS AFTERMATH

After first recoiling from Hitler's advances,[3] the Red Army came into its own, which included Latvia, Esthonia, Lithuania, Rumania, Bulgaria, Czechoslovakia, Hungary, Albania, East Germany, and Poland. On August 8, 1945, Stalin brought the

[1] Two years later, but this was the slow-drying kind.
[2] See also Finland's attack on Russia and South Korea's attack on North Korea.
[3] Who wouldn't?

Soviet into the war with Japan and humbled the Mikado [1] in less than a week, and without fighting. This was a considerable improvement over the nineteen months it took Russia to be defeated by Japan in 1904–05.

In the closing years of the war, Stalin met twice with Churchill and Roosevelt. Just as he felt he could hold his

Trying each other's smokes

inscrutable smile no longer, the Allies tricked him by sending in a new team, Attlee and Truman. This pair was entirely different from the first, Attlee not caring for cigars and Truman possessing neither a cape nor a cigarette holder. Stalin wondered who had assassinated those other fellows.

Little was accomplished, save that the American and British, though notoriously poor linguists, finally grasped the meaning

[1] Slaughtered the Pirates of Penzance, too.

of the Russian word, *"Nyet!"* [1] The heads of state spent most of the time having their pictures taken and comparing scars. (Stalin showed his stubborn streak.) At Potsdam, Stalin clapped for an orderly just as Truman finished playing "The Missouri Waltz," and instead of a drink got an encore.

Music lovers

At these sessions, so many toasts were proposed (and accepted) that drinking became a problem, although there were no problem drinkers. Churchill slyly soaked up his drinks in his cigar, Truman dumped his into the piano, and Stalin is thought to have had a small storage tank under his mustache. In one way or another the conferees managed to keep their eyes clear even when their intentions were not.

After the war it was assumed that Stalin would help his former allies keep the peace. He was affectionately called Uncle Joe by almost everyone, and the Kremlin became known as Uncle Joe's Cabin. But Stalin had not forgotten his pledge of allegiance to the hammer and sickle "and to the revolution for which it stands." It was not by accident that his agents could be spotted in the Trouble Spots of the world, ostensibly working as caviar salesmen. Nor did the perishability of caviar ex-

[1] N(ot)yet.

plain why it had to be packed in gun barrels for shipment to China and the Middle East. Stalin had something up his sleeves, probably arms.

THE SATELLITES

Russian rulers had always felt their country to be surrounded by enemies. Stalin hit upon a novel way to remedy this situation. By taking over all the adjoining countries, he would surround Russia with Russia! To achieve his goal, he first encouraged all the small nations bordering on Russia to elect Communist governments. One form of encouragement was to provide large numbers of Russian soldiers to help get out the vote. Persons needing transportation to the polls would be conveyed by trucks or, if they wanted to be sure to get safely through the traffic, by tanks. Also provided were trained ballot counters. There was nothing Stalin wouldn't do for a neighbor.

These countries became known as satellites and had puppet governments which kept the people entertained with Punch and Judy shows. One of the advantages of being a satellite was that

Getting out the vote

there was a favorable balance of trade. Wheat, machinery, and dirty old factories could be palmed off on Russia in return for brand-new pictures of Stalin and autographed copies of his *History of the Communist Party of the Soviet Union.*

There was also a boom in tourism in the satellites. Soviet officials made all-expense tours [1] of these countries to review troops, sample food, and buy wrist watches. When the wine had been tested by aides who were considered expendable, toasts were drunk to the everlasting friendship and trust between the two nations.

COMMUNISM IN AMERICA AND ASIA

Stalin hoped, as had Lenin, to spread Communism throughout the world. In America his purpose was served by *The Daily Worker,* which carried on its masthead the motto: "All the news that fits, we print." It could reverse its position on an issue on twenty-four hours' notice. This maneuver became known as the flip-flop because the American editors flipped when a Russian policy flopped. The Communist Party in America was inexplicably led for some years by a titled gentleman, Earl Browder. Histories of American Communism make frequent references to the Communist Front but remain discreetly silent about the Communist Behind.

In Asia someone coined the phrase, "Asia for the Asiatics." [2] Signs reading "Down With Yankee Right Fielders" appeared in great numbers, and crowds in the streets of Tientsin shouted: "Amelican Malines, So Long." Stalin had set up sign factories and schools for demonstration directors from Peiping to Hongkong. The leader, after sounding a tuning fork for pitch and waving his arms a few times for tempo, would melt into the crowd, especially on a hot day.

In 1950, Stalin and the leader of Communist China, Mao Tse-tung (with tung in cheek), signed a thirty-year friendship pact, both of them politely refraining from any mention of

[1] All expenses paid by the country visited.
[2] See also "Amnesia for the Amnesiacs."

Two for tea

Stalin's pact with Hitler in 1939. Stalin, who was in his seventy-first year, had reason to doubt that he would be around when the thirty years were up.

THE DOCTORS' PLOT

Early in 1953 nine Soviet doctors were arrested. They were accused of not discovering Salk Vaccine and not founding the Mayo Clinic. Having lost four out of five of their patients, many of them high-ranking Party members, they were suspected of incompetence. One was said to have tried to examine a patient's fallen arches by peering through his bronchial tubes. Another was accused of attempting to mend a punctured lung with a rubber patch and a vulcanizing kit. In a brilliant defense, this doctor referred to the patient's lungs as her "inner tubes" and almost won acquittal.

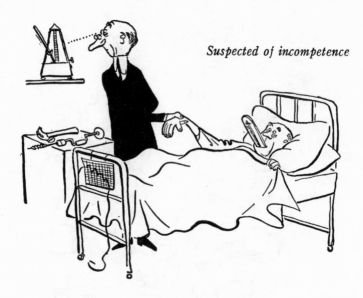

Suspected of incompetence

This so-called Doctors' Plot, named after the area in the cemetery reserved for their patients, led to a trial which was widely attended by people who hoped to pick up some medical advice free. All nine doctors were given a dose of their own medicine and put in prison where the effects could be observed. A few years later they were freed and decorated with the Legion of Decency and the Order of Hippocrates.

DEATH OF STALIN

On March 5, 1953, the Moscow radio announced that Stalin had died of a stroke. Those who had come to think of him as a god were forced to revise their thinking.[1] There was a rumor that the radio reports were tardy and that Stalin had been dead for weeks. The reason for the delay was that the embalmer was having trouble making him look as good as Lenin. After all, if the two great men were to lie side by side in the mausoleum on Red Square, there should be no invidious comparisons.

[1] Downward.

At Stalin's funeral, speeches were made by the three top Party members, G. M. ("General Motors") Malenkov, L. P. ("Long Playing") Beria, and V. M. ("Vyacheslav Mikhailovich") Molotov. They remembered that Stalin had made the principal oration at Lenin's funeral, and had become head man. So they vied with each other to outpraise their deceased leader, hailing him as "the heir of Lenin" and "the interpreter of Marx." Because of limitations of time, no mention was made of Stalin's career as a bank robber or as a liquidator of old comrades.

The death of Stalin marked the end of an era and, even more conclusively, the end of Stalin. Lying in his tomb alongside Lenin, he could be sure of one final achievement. Those who waited patiently in line would now see a double feature.

CHAPTER VIII

AFTER STALIN

NO ONE EXPECTED Georgi Malenkov to succeed Stalin. How could a man only five feet seven who weighed over 250 pounds and was known by his friends as Fatsovich lead Russia anywhere except to the dinner table? Would his speeches to underfed workers sound convincing? But stranger things have happened, although none comes to mind at the moment.[1]

MALENKOV'S RISE

Little as the world knew about Malenkov in 1953, he had already made a place for himself in the Communist Party. His

---

[1] After a visit to Malenkov, a Czech diplomat described him as looking "exactly like a Turkish eunuch." This was not a very diplomatic remark.

biographer says that he won his spurs as a Commissar on the Turkestan front during the Civil War. Having won his spurs, he was never without them, as Party work horses had good reason to know. A man of refinement and taste, his brass knuckles were always fastidiously polished and bore the initials "G. M."

Malenkov was a protégé of Stalin's, becoming a member of his private secretariat and achieving a position of confidence (in his survival) during the 1937–38 purges. It was Malenkov whom Stalin asked to examine the lists of those about to be purged, to see whether anyone had been slighted. Malenkov was also one of the few whom Stalin invited to the Kremlin for an evening of looking through his photograph album at old friends who were no more.

What gave Malenkov real power was being managing director of ORPO, or in other (longer) words, Otdel Rukovodia- shchikh Partiinikh Organov. As such, he kept track of all the important Party members and reported directly to Stalin which ones were still alive and why. In this job he learned that the way to get ahead was not to have your name in the headlines but to keep it out of the obituary column.

So it was that, when Stalin died, Malenkov stepped into his shoes, which were still warm.

MALENKOV AS PREMIER

Malenkov at once proclaimed a policy of coexistence. He could see no reason why Communist Russia and what in a generous moment he called "the Fascist Barbarians of the West," could not live side by side, or even back to back. He also demanded a rise in consumer goods, especially foodstuffs, because now that he was Premier he really intended to stuff himself.

One casualty during Malenkov's premiership was Lavrenti P. Beria, Minister of the Interior. As his title suggests, it was his job to look inside of houses, desk drawers, personal letters, and people. He also was head of the secret police, and had only

Intended to stuff himself

to snap his fingers or crack his knuckles and his men would jump out from the molding and do their grim duty.

Beria had been one of Malenkov's staunchest supporters, always at hand to prop up his friend after a heavy dinner. But, as one historian has said, "he knew too much." Malenkov couldn't stand having anyone around who was better informed than he. So Beria was relieved of his office, shot, and tried.

But Malenkov didn't last long as Premier. Within two years, on February 8, 1955, he appeared before the Supreme Soviet and made an eloquent speech, the gist of which was that he was completely disgusted with himself. The applause was deafening. He said his agricultural program had failed, there was a shortage of radishes, and his salad days were over. The standard of living instead of rising had declined, and there was now an average of only 2.4 chairs per family. He was inexperienced, incompetent, irrelevant,[1] and he hated himself. At this point his voice broke, and in the silence that ensued before it could be mended, his resignation was accepted.

Everyone expected Malenkov to be liquidated, in his case melted down for tallow. But someone had a brilliant idea. Why

[1] Some thought he said "irreverent" and wondered what all the fuss was about.

Minister of the Interior

not make him Minister of Electric Power Stations and send him out to inspect high-voltage lines? This was done, and everyone laid in a supply of candles, expecting a temporary short circuit. Electrocution being more humane than shooting, it was obvious that the old days of Czarist and Communist brutality were over.

COLLECTIVE LEADERSHIP

The governing body now came to have two heads. The first time people noticed it they thought they had been drinking too much. Nikolai Bulganin took over Malenkov's job as Premier and Nikita Khrushchev took over his job as Secretary of the Central Committee, thus improving the employment situation and spearheading a Back-to-Work or One-Man-to-a-Job movement. By means of a new system called Collective Leadership or Share-the-Blame, the government was broadened to include Malenkov, Molotov, and Lazar Kaganovich. Thus when leaders were accused of bungling, they could simply shrug their shoulders and point at each other. It was only when an honor was to be bestowed that there was any difficulty.

Collective leadership

Bulganin and Khrushchev, affectionately known as Bulge and Krutch, set off on a series of tours to China, Yugoslavia,[1] India, and England, to prove that Russia was no bugbear, or at least a bugbear that walked like a man. Everywhere they went they talked with workers, which they did not do in Russia for fear of slowing down production. Once their facial muscles became accustomed to it, both men smiled broadly and incessantly and came to be known as Jolly Good Fellows. Khrushchev was the one who did most of the talking and most of the drinking, and the more he did of the latter the more he did of the former.

At the Twentieth Party Congress, in February, 1956, Khrushchev made a seven-hour speech which left his hearers amazed.[2] He accused Stalin of despotism, greed, megalomania,

[1] Where Tito was blowing hot and cold, a feat which it was worth traveling a thousand miles to see.

[2] And sore, unless they had the foresight to bring cushions.

incompetence, arrogance, and biting his fingernails. Khrushchev admitted that he should have revealed these facts years before, but he had been too polite to mention them while Stalin was alive and they had somehow slipped his mind for the past three years.

Thus came the end of the Cult of Personality and the beginning of a period of de-Stalinization. Every day people were to shrink their portraits of Stalin a little and whittle away at his statues until he was cut down to size. Battalions of sign painters were recruited to change names of streets and cities. Stalin Prizes and Stalin Medals, along with empty vodka bottles, could be turned in for a small cash refund.

Jolly good fellows

ONE BOSS AGAIN

But Collective Leadership died young. One Day Khrushchev was walking down the street arm in arm with Malenkov, Molotov, and Kaganovich, chatting amiably. The next day he rose before the Central Committee [1] and accused these Com-

[1] He must have been an early riser, or else the rest of them slept late.

rades of all manner of heinous crimes. "No man is too big for the Party," he snarled, looking straight at Malenkov, who was sitting on three chairs. Molotov and Kaganovich likewise came in for some uncomplimentary remarks, and might better have remained outside. Obviously their friendship had paled, perhaps because of those months in the Kremlin with the blinds drawn.

With a friend like Khrushchev, they didn't need any enemies

Whatever the reason, the three men were dropped from their high offices, though not, like some satellite leaders, via their windows. Malenkov was sent to run a power station in East Kazakhstan, it being hoped that this time he really *would* stick his finger in a light socket. Molotov was made Ambassador to Mongolia, as a test case to see whether diplomatic immunity would afford any protection against yellow fever. Kaganovich was assigned to a cement factory in Sverdlovsk, Western Siberia, and was likely to be stuck there indefinitely.

Shortly afterward Marshal Zhukov, who had helped Khrushchev get rid of the others, was rewarded by being relieved of his onerous duties as Defense Minister and head of the Red Army. Those present when he learned of his reassignment to a desk job [1] say that he wept tears of gratitude and beat his chest

[1] Inspector of Paper Clips and Pencil Sharpeners.

Zhukov rewarded

until he jarred loose two rows of medals. As for Khrushchev, he now felt free to revive the Cult of Personality, which had lost some of its former repulsiveness, and writers of history books wearily began revising their just-completed revisions.

AN UNEXPECTED TRIUMPH

One afternoon Khrushchev was sitting at his desk in the Kremlin, idly drawing Russian doodles (something like Yankee doodles) on a scratch pad. Now and then he whirled around in his swivel chair (a revolutionary Russian invention), trying to simulate the feeling he got from a slug of vodka.

A man, claiming to be an inventor, had been trying for days to get an audience with the Party Chief. He had something of great urgency to tell him, and would disclose it to no one else. Finally Khrushchev said to send him in, he would hear him out. (Some thought he said "heave him out.")

The inventor, a bald-headed little man named Stanislav V. Sputnik, put before Khrushchev a fantastic proposal. If Khrushchev would give him the funds and two dozen German ___ he could send a rocket to the moon and make it a ___ gary and Czechoslovakia.

___ nought the man was off his rocker, but he ___ ded another satellite. There hadn't been a new one since Syria. So he sent Sputnik to Ulrich von Hacken-schmertz with a note that read: "Of course it's impossible. But if you and Sputnik hit the moon, I'll let you work in your laboratory without leg irons."

The rest is history. Sputnik and Hackenschmertz launched a missile for the moon. Through a miscalculation, or a power failure, it got up only a few hundred miles, then leveled off and began zooming crazily around the earth. When the bad news came to Khrushchev, who had been peering through binoculars at the moon for hours, he buried his face in his hands and sobbed. He should never have let that stupid Sputnik go ahead. Russian science would be the laughingstock of the world. "Somebody shoot the damned thing down, for the love of Lenin," he screamed. "And shoot the inventor too!"

Then a wonderful thing happened. Cablegrams of praise began to pour in. Every nation wanted a "Sputnik" of its own overhead, going around and around like mad and getting nowhere. By unbalancing its budget and straining every sinew, the United States after a couple of hectic months got a Sputnik into the sky, whizzing around in the approved manner. Soon country after country, from England to Liechtenstein, was plunging into debt to have a Sputnik it could call its very own.

Khrushchev, though at first incredulous, soon realized that by a brilliant decision he had achieved Communism's greatest victory. He summoned Comrade Sputnik, and none too soon. When Khrushchev's message arrived, the firing squad had already fired and the bullets were in mid-flight. A second later and they would have passed the point of no return. Sputnik was hurried to the Kremlin, still blindfolded and clutching his slide rule. There he was embraced by Khrushchev, who kissed him on both cheeks and made him a Folk Hero with Oak Leaf Cluster. While Sputnik stood there with a puzzled look on his face, still trying to figure out what had gone wrong with his calculations, Khrushchev pinned medals on him from his collar to his trouser cuffs.

Khrushchev was beside himself. Neither Lenin nor Stali

Comrade Sputnik becomes a Folk Hero

had pulled off anything like this. Peasants and workers might not be eating any better, but they could look up into the sky and say, "It's ours, all ours." Khrushchev was shrewd enough not to tell them it belonged to the State, just as they did.

Though holding only the title of First Secretary of the Central Committee of the Communist Party, Khrushchev was now unquestionably top dog.[1]

A FEW FINAL WORDS

And so we bring the story of Communism to the present, which is as far as we can safely go. By way of review, we remind the reader that Marx never did have much hope for Russia, that Lenin, Trotsky, and Stalin have gone down in history under assumed names, and that Khrushchev rode to glory on a slight miscalculation in azimuth.

[1] Except for the one in Sputnik II. Soon afterward, when Bulganin left the government for a position in a bank, with shorter hours and longer life expectancy, Khrushchev became Premier.

As we look back over the Bolsheviks and the Mensheviks, the Whites and the Reds, the purgers and the purged, we must leave the reader with one final thought. There are those who feel a certain nostalgia for the good old days of Ivan the Terrible, who had never read Marx and had no use for the proletariat. At least you could go to bed at night and wake up in the morning, secure in the knowledge of whom to hate.

ABOUT THE AUTHOR

Richard Armour has never been to Russia, does not speak Russian, and does not wear a beard, even in the dead of winter. He has never been before a Senatorial committee, nor has he ever been an agent for the FBI. Far from having led three lives, he is slightly behind in one.

Nevertheless he prepared himself for this study of Russia and Communism to a remarkable degree—i.e., a Harvard Ph.D. in English philology, which enables him to quote the Lord's Prayer in Gothic. Now that the Goths have died out, there are very few who can do this. Many years of teaching English literature at such institutions as Northwestern University, the University of Texas, Wells College, the University of Freiburg, and the University of Hawaii have forced him to learn to read. His students remember him for his searching questions, such as "Where did I put my glasses case?"

His books, of which this is the eighteenth, have brought him legions of admirers, including the American Legion, the Foreign Legion, and the Legion of Decency, which keeps hoping for improvement. He writes in both prose and verse, though not simultaneously, and is known for his resounding periods as well as his delicately curving commas.

Richard Armour teaches at Scripps College, a college for women. He enjoys his work.

ABOUT THE ILLUSTRATOR

Campbell Grant, who has illustrated five of Richard Armour's books, is not hung in any of the great galleries of the world, for which he is grateful. Nonetheless he was one of Walt Disney's top artists for twelve years, and during World War II dared shot and shell in Hollywood, working with Frank Capra on documentaries. Since his ignorance of Russian history and Communism is matched only by that of the author, he was perfectly equipped to do the drawings for the present book. Grant lives on a ranch near Santa Barbara, California, where, with the help of his wife, he raises avocados and children.